John Filson of Kentucke

JOHN FILSON

Colonel Reuben T. Durrett had this portrait painted from a sketch on the flyleaf of *Admonitions from the Dead in Epistles to the Living,* owned by Filson. The unknown artist may have been Aurelius O. Revenaugh or Nicola Marschall. The portrait is now owned by the Filson Club, Louisville.

John Filson

OF KENTUCKE

By John Walton

LEXINGTON KENTUCKY

Printed at the University of Kentucky

Library of Congress Catalog Card No. 56-6995

Publication of this book is possible partly by reason of a grant from the Margaret Voorhies Haggin Trust established in memory of her husband James Ben Ali Haggin

To Elizabeth Keene Walton

Preface

BIOGRAPHY is both history and literature. Writing on the subject recently, Sir Harold Nicolson enumerated three principles that the serious biographer should observe: a biography must be accurate and depict a person in relation to his time; it must describe an individual with all the gradations of human character; and it must be written in grammatical English and with an adequate feeling for style. In writing this life of John Filson I have tried to be faithful to these canons.

That biography should portray a distinctive individual has been an easy principle to follow. Filson was a frontiersman, but it would be impossible to fit him into that stereotype; he was a pedagogue, but he was not a typical one; and he possessed both virtues and vices without representing a type of either.

To relate Filson to his contemporary world has been more difficult. The historian is at the mercy of chance for the quantity and credibility of his evidence; and in this case the paucity of the materials—Filson had only five years of activity, and those were on the frontier—has been a handicap. However, he was unmistakably a child of late eighteenth century America, nurtured by the optimism, the ambition, and the romanticism of the period. Moving in the first great tide of immigration that flowed westward through the Appalachian valleys, he became a frontiersman in his own right. Despite his pedantry, or perhaps because of it, he was a useful member of this crowd of explorers, empire builders, soldiers, gentlemen, pilgrims, heretics, refugees, criminals, escapists, and dreamers. He grabbed land along with the most rapacious of them, and by his writing he promoted its settlement. As the architect of the Boone legend, he created the prototype of the American hero. And as a wandering schoolmaster, he was one of the first to spread light and learning on the frontier. These things I have tried to show as I have related the brief and swiftly moving narrative of his life.

The character of the subject of a biography is bound to influence the style in which it is written. The restlessness of Filson has been contagious, speeding up the normal tempo of the writing; and the floridity of his own work has doubtless left a subtle and pervasive impress on an otherwise academic style. Furthermore, it would have been impossible, even had it been desirable, to avoid the inherent melodrama in the story of this guileless little schoolmaster, clutching vainly at the extravagant promises of the frontier. Whether the style is appropriate and adequate is a question for the reader to decide.

Whatever inaccuracies and misinterpretations appear are due solely to my own limitations as a scholar, for I have enjoyed unusual co-operation from those who possess the fragmentary records of Filson's life. It would be impossible to list all the persons to whom I am indebted. However, it would be a greater injustice not to mention any of them. To all of them I am grateful, and particularly to J. Winston Coleman, Jr., of Lexington, Kentucky, and J. M. Stephens of the Johns Hopkins University, Baltimore, Maryland, both of whom have given me help, encouragement, and criticism; and to Richard H. Hill of the Filson Club, Louisville, Kentucky, Bart Anderson of the Chester County Historical Society, West Chester, Pennsylvania, Miss Ruthanna Hindes of the Historical Society of Wilmington, Delaware, Miss Jacqueline Bull of the University of Kentucky Library, Lexington, Virginius Hall and Mrs. Alice Hook of the Ohio Historical and Philosophical Society, Cincinnati, R. N. Williams, II, of the Historical Society of Pennsylvania, Malcolm Young of the Princeton University Library, Henry Howard Eddy of the Pennsylvania Historical and Museum Commission, Dr. Beulah Tatum of the Johns Hopkins University, William J. Van Schreeven, State Archivist of Virginia, the staffs at the Enoch Pratt and Peabody libraries in Baltimore, and countless others who have contributed to the completion of the manuscript.

JOHN WALTON

February 22, 1955
Baltimore, Maryland

Contents

Illustrations

Introduction

IT IS INDEED ironic that Kentucky's first historian and cartographer, the man who discovered Daniel Boone and quickly spread his name and exploits to distant parts of the world, advertising in colors wonderfully bright the new country which would be forever associated with that intrepid pioneer, should have had so little written about himself!

From that day 168 years ago, when the young, adventurous John Filson met his tragic and untimely death in the somber canebrakes of the western wilderness while surveying the site of a town he named Losantiville—now Cincinnati—until the publication of the present volume, no thorough, critical study had ever been made of his short but eventful and fruitful life which an unkind fate had seemed to consign to near oblivion.

Now, happily it may be said that with this full-length, carefully written, amply documented biography—starkly scrupulous in its factual recital—this almost forgotten man to whom America is so deeply indebted finally has "come into his own."

It is both fortunate and eminently fitting that this arduous task should have been undertaken by John Walton, whose family lines run deep in the stock of Kentucky pioneers. A graduate of that first institution of higher learning west of the Alleghenies—Transylvania College—he is also an alumnus of the University of Kentucky. Receiving his doctorate at the

Johns Hopkins University in Baltimore, he is now a member of its faculty.

As the great-great-grandson of Samuel Filson, an early settler in Kentucky and a cousin of John Filson, the author grew up with a deep-seated conviction that his early and somewhat pathetic kinsman someday should emerge from more than a century of obscurity to occupy his rightful place in American history.

This doubtless explains the unflagging interest which has sustained him so resolutely in his long and difficult quest for the authentic facts—so elusive and widely scattered as they have proved to be—relating to his subject and the activities of that brief and restless career.

That Dr. Walton has achieved a goal even perhaps beyond his most sanguine expectations is abundantly evident from only a casual perusal of this volume. It is a distinct contribution to American biography and to frontier history, accurately and absorbingly related. I wish and predict for it the success which it so richly deserves at the hands of all readers who are interested in history, exploration, and high adventure.

J. Winston Coleman, Jr.

January 15, 1956
Winburn Farm
Lexington, Kentucky

Chapter 1 Backgrounds

JOHN FILSON was born about 1753 on the banks of the Brandywine in Chester County, Pennsylvania, and he disappeared thirty-five years later in the sycamore forests along the Great Miami River in southern Ohio. His name, however, has been remembered with that of Kentucky; in fact they are mutually indebted for their fame. If there had been no Kentucky, Filson might easily have died in the same obscurity in which he passed his early years; and if there had been no Filson, Kentucky would not have been so favorably known on two continents. The trail from the Brandywine to the Bluegrass was a perilous one, but Filson chose to follow it. This biography is one of the remote consequences of that choice.

The Filson family were among the many Scotch-Irish settlers who came from Ulster to Pennsylvania during the early part of the eighteenth century. According to some historians, the family was English,[1] but this error probably originated with a statement by Colonel Reuben Durrett, Filson's first biographer, that the Filsons were among the "English-speaking" families who succeeded the Swedes in the rich and beautiful valley of the Brandywine.[2] In addition to the circumstantial evidence—the name, their neighbors, and their Presbyterianism—there is a fairly consistent tradition that the Filsons are of Ulster origin. A Chester County historian published a sketch of Filson's ancestry in 1887, and although he apparently drew heavily on Durrett's biography for much of his information, he stated that the family was Scotch-Irish:

> The Filson family were of Scotch-Irish origin, and on their emigration to this country settled in East Fallowfield Township, at and around where the old Doe Run Presbyterian Church now stands, on the Strasburg road. The emigrant ancestor of the family in this country was John Filson, the grandfather of the subject of this sketch. He came over prior to 1740, as in this year he and others, associated with him, were instrumental in the organization of the Doe Run Presbyterian Church, and the erection of its first place of worship on the grounds, and near to the site of the present buildings.[3]

Furthermore, there is a strong tradition in the family that they are "Irish."[4]

Lacking documentary proof of an Ulster origin, one is compelled to substantiate the tradition by the available circumstantial evidence. The name Filson, especially in its variant form, Philson, is indicative of the provenance of the family. As early as 1469, one Fergusius or Fargus Philsone resided in Aberdeen.[5] Obviously this spelling is another form of Phillips and Phillipson, both frequently found in Scotland and Ulster. Among the residents of the latter, lavish use was made of the patronymic *son;* and one finds innumerable Adamsons, Atkinsons, Andersons, Carsons, Davidsons, Gibsons, Gilkisons, Don-

1 Willard Rouse Jillson wrote "his [John Filson's] father, Davison Filson, and his mother being of thrifty English farming stock." *Filson's Kentucke* (Filson Club *Publications,* no. 35, Louisville, 1930), 139. Also in Marshall W. Fishwick, "Daniel Boone and the Pattern of the Western Hero," *Filson Club History Quarterly,* XXVII (1953), 124: "Filson was the grandson of an English immigrant," and in the *Dictionary of American Biography,* VI, 382.

2 *John Filson, the First Historian of Kentucky* (Filson Club *Publications,* no. 1, Louisville, 1884), 7.

3 J. Smith Futhey, in West Chester, Pa., *Village Record,* March 10, 1887.

4 Joseph Beatty Doyle, *History of Steubenville and Jefferson County* (Chicago, Twentieth Century, Richmond-Arnold Publishing Co., 1910), 639-40.

5 George Fraser Black, *The Surnames of Scotland* (New York Public Library, 1946), 660.

aldsons, Hendersons, Jamisons, Jacksons, Johnsons, Morrisons, Robinsons, Pattersons, Stephensons, Thompsons, and Wilsons among the Scotch-Irish immigrants to this country. The usual patronymic for Philip, however, is *s*,[6] a form characteristic of Welsh and west-of-England names, although not lacking among the Scots.[7] Phillipson also occurs; and in this instance, apparently a rare one, Philson, which became Filson.

As Ulster immigrants to America, the Filson family were moving in a great Völkerwanderung of the western world. The Ulstermen who came to this country were almost invariably referred to as "Irishmen" by the English settlers, but they regarded themselves as Scots who had been sojourners in the North of Ireland. They were not Irish, and for a time at least, they hoped to preserve the distinction. As one Ulster Scot rejoined, "If a man is born in a stable does that make him a horse?"[8] Originally most of them had been Lowland Scots and of the same complicated lineage as the English immediately south of them. The blood of the Celts, Romans, Frisians, Angles, Saxons, Danes, Norwegians, Normans, and Flemings had been compounded in their veins for centuries. Early in the seventeenth century they began their wandering, and they

6 There are thirty-three Phillips in the Ulster Telephone Directory today, but no Filsons.

7 Alexander, a favorite Scots name, has both Sanderson and Saunders as patronymic variants.

8 Quoted in Wayland F. Dunaway, *The Scotch-Irish of Colonial Pennsylvania* (Chapel Hill, University of North Carolina Press, 1944), 8, an authorized publication of the Pennsylvania Scotch-Irish Society. The general information about the Scotch-Irish in this chapter has been obtained from Dunaway and the following sources: Charles A. Hanna, *The Scotch-Irish or the Scot in North Britain, North Ireland, and North America* (2 vols., New York, G. P. Putnam's Sons, 1902); Maude Glasgow, *The Scotch-Irish in Northern Ireland and in the American Colonies* (New York, G. P. Putnam's Sons, 1936); Henry James Ford, *The Scotch-Irish in America* (Princeton University Press, 1913); "The Settlement of Ulster," *Edinburgh Review,* CXXIX (1869), 419-54; Cyril Falls, *The Birth of Ulster* (London, Methuen & Company, 1936); James Anthony Froude, *The English in Ireland in the Eighteenth Century* (3 vols., London, Longmans, Green & Company, 1901); and John P. Prendergast, *The Cromwellian Settlement of Ireland* (London, Longman, Green, Longman, Roberts and Green, 1865).

have continued almost until the present. Before the reign of James I they began moving from Scotland to the counties of Antrim and Down across the North Channel; and by 1610 they were pouring into the six "escheated" counties—Armagh, Fermanagh, Tyrone, Londonderry, Cavan, and Donegal—which had passed from the control of the Irish earls into the hands of the Crown. Some of Cromwell's soldiers joined them in the early 1650's, and there was a sprinkling of French Huguenots in the land. Although alone they could have preserved the purity of their faith, these Scottish Calvinists found allies among a population that was predominately Catholic. Perhaps they became somewhat less provincial and clannish as they joined the French and the English in reclaiming the soil of the province, but they set their stamp on Ulster. With characteristic energy they transformed the desolation of Northern Ireland into a garden, developed the distinctive "plantation" culture, and started the industry of the province on its way.[9]

By 1700 the second phase of the great migration had begun. The obvious reasons for this movement were political, economic, and religious; but the men of Ulster were a restless lot even under favorable conditions, often driven by inner compulsion as well as by circumstance. Apparently feeling no need for the assurance of familiar scenes, they migrated easily.[10] Their patriotism was an allegiance to the ideals of freedom rather than a sentimental attachment to familiar landmarks; and their religious faith, expressed in the Presbyterian Church militant, did not require the palpable textures and ancient

[9] For a popular account of the development of Ulster, see Denis O'D. Hanna, *The Face of Ulster* (London, Batsford, 1952).

[10] Thornton Wilder, in describing the character of the first immigrants to America, wrote: "Their sense of identity did not derive from their relation to their environment. The meaning which their lives had for them was inner and individual. They did not need to be supported, framed, consoled, by the known, the habitual, the loved, by the ancestral village, by the air, sky and water that they knew." In "Toward an American Language," *Atlantic Monthly,* cxc (July, 1952), 32.

impedimenta of the more sensuous faiths. A practical common sense prevented them from sinking illogical roots in any land, and their self-reliance was an antidote for fear of the unknown.

Of the series of events that conspired to drive the Ulster Scots to America, three affected them economically, and the fourth, equally intolerable, interfered with their religion. In 1699 the English placed restrictions on Irish trade;[11] in 1717 the original land leases began to expire and could be renewed only by paying twice or thrice the original rent—a practice known as rack-renting;[12] and in 1727, 1740, and 1770 there were widespread famines in Ireland. Added to these vexations was the hateful Test Act that required all civil and military officers to take Communion in the Church of England.[13] The English aroused the lasting ire of the Ulstermen by irritating him at the two points where he was extremely sensitive—his purse and his kirk. They were to meet him again on the remote battlefields of the American Revolution.

From the ports of Belfast and Newry, Strangford and Ballycastle, Londonderry and Larne, 250,000 Scotch-Irish sailed for America.[14] They settled in every one of the thirteen original colonies; but Pennsylvania with its reputation for liberality and tolerance attracted the majority of them. By 1710 they had settled at Fagg's Manor, Upper Octorara, and Brandywine Manor in Chester County, "the first nursery" of the Scotch-Irish in this country. As they continued to come in ever increasing numbers, Penn's government made them attractive land offers in the Cumberland Valley, where they might provide a *cordon sanitaire* against the Indians.[15] The Scotch-Irish readily accepted the invitation to move into unsettled wilderness. The Friends, exclusive, pietistic, peculiar, and English, were in control along the seaboard; and immediately to the

[11] Froude, I, 292-98. [12] Glasgow, 155. [13] Dunaway, 30-33. [14] *Ibid.*

[15] Isaac Sharpless, *A History of Quaker Government in Pennsylvania* (2 vols., Philadelphia, T. S. Leach & Co., 1900), II, 9.

west the Germans, alien in language and custom, had already pre-empted the good land. Opportunity for the new settlers lay farther to the west.

Not long after the first smoke had risen from the chimneys of their cabins in the Cumberland Valley, another great dispersion of the Scotch-Irish began. These westward-walking men poured into Maryland, down the Valley of Virginia, and into the uplands of the South. As early as 1719 they were at Martinsburg;[16] in 1734 at Harper's Ferry;[17] and not much later they were the dominant element in Augusta, Rockbridge, and Botetourt counties in Virginia.[18] From there they spread south to the Waxhaws and fanned out westward into western Pennsylvania, Kentucky, and Tennessee.

When the War of the Revolution came, the Scotch-Irish showed almost complete unanimity in their sympathy with the cause of the colonies. There were no Tories among them.

> And when the days of trial came
> Of which we know the story
> No Erin son of Scotia's blood
> Was ever found a Tory.[19]

At least twice they had anticipated the Declaration of Independence by similar declarations of their own,[20] and they joined

16 Hanna, II, 45.

17 See the list of genealogies in J. Lewis Peyton, *History of Augusta County, Virginia* (Staunton, S. M. Yost & Son, 1882), 302-12.

18 The attraction of cheaper land and lower taxes in the Shenandoah Valley was one of the reasons for the movement of the Germans and the Scotch-Irish into the Valley of Virginia. George Maclaren Brydon, *Virginia's Mother Church* (Richmond, Virginia Historical Society, 1947), 154.

19 By Mrs. Samuel Evans; quoted in Dunaway, 155.

20 One signed at Hanna's Town, Pennsylvania, on May 16, 1775. See George Dallas Albert, *The Frontier Forts of Western Pennsylvania* (Pennsylvania Indian Forts Commission, *Report,* II [2d ed., Harrisburg, W. S. Ray, 1916]), 294-96. The second was the famous Mecklenburg Declaration in North Carolina, or more accurately the Mecklenburg Resolves, May 31, 1775, for which see William L. Saunders (ed.), *The Colonial Records of North Carolina* (10 vols., Raleigh, P. M. Hale, 1886-1890), IX, 1282-85.

eagerly with the other colonists in the war against the familiar tyranny. Having proved themselves at Bannockburn, at Inniskillen, and at Londonderry,[21] they were no mean fighting men. They had fought with the wild Scottish Highlanders, with the wild Irish, and with the wild American Indians.[22] There was not the slightest vein of pacificism anywhere in their culture. In the war with England they fought as privates, sergeants, ensigns, and captains; they recruited and furnished supplies, when they had them, to the continental troops; and, although the fire of their enthusiasm for the cause of the colonies flickered at times, it never did so out of sympathy for the English.

These restless rangers on American frontiers were not irresponsible vagrants escaping from the restraints and responsibilities of the civilized community, nor were they mere squatters looking for an easy, simple, adventurous life. They were, for the most part, men of strong political and religious convictions. Moreover, they were men of incomparable physical vigor. Lord Roseberry has expressed without reserve his good opinion of their virtues: "We know that the term Ulster Scot is generic and simply means Scoto-Irish. I love the Highlander and I love the Lowlander, but when I come to that branch of our race which has been grafted on to the Ulster stem, I take off my hat with veneration and awe. They are, I believe, the toughest, the most dominant, the most irresistible race that exists in the universe at this moment."[23] In them a belief in human action combined paradoxically with an intense and deterministic religious faith. If they were not fatalists, they at least accepted the larger mechanism of destiny; but at the same time they put their trust in their own ability to work out

21 Dunaway, 143.

22 Toynbee traces their migration and their battles with a succession of hostile neighbors. His interpretation of their failure in the southern highlands of the United States is open to question, however. See Arnold J. Toynbee, *A Study of History* (10 vols., London, Oxford University Press, 1934-1954), II, 309-13.

23 Quoted in Dunaway, 13.

their earthly salvation. If they believed that all outcomes were predetermined, they worked with unremitting energy to bring them about. Presbyterian almost to a man when they came to America, many of them later became Baptists, Methodists, and Disciples of Christ. As Scots they tended to be inflexible, dogmatic, and doctrinaire; and although the grim faith of Scotland had been somewhat softened by the verdure of Ireland and broadened by the expanse of the American continent, it remained a religion of abstraction and contention. Not only did it spawn new sects, but within the fold Presbyterianism was continually splintering into many fragments. There are and have been Presbyterians Old Side and New Side, Associate Reformed Presbyterians and just Reformed Presbyterians, Covenanters and Cumberlanders, and Presbyterians of the United States of America and Presbyterians of the United States.[24]

With them religion and learning went hand in hand; and their factionalism in the eighteenth century encouraged an increase in the number of Presbyterian schools.[25] At Fagg's Manor the Scotch-Irish had a classical school, and at Neshaminy a log college. In 1744 they established Nottingham Academy at Colora, Maryland, which is still being run by the Presbyterian Church. In nearly every frontier community where they settled, these people of the Book built academies which often became colleges.[26] Princeton University is a successor to one of their log colleges; and in western Pennsylvania they built Washington and Jefferson; in Virginia, Washington and Lee; in Kentucky, Transylvania; and in North Carolina, Davidson. Their influence in the state universities was so great that Jef-

[24] William Warren Sweet (ed.), *Religion on the American Frontier,* II: *The Presbyterians, 1783-1840* (New York, Harper and Brothers, 1936), 6.

[25] For documentary materials on the contention between the Old Siders and the New Siders, see L. H. Butterfield (ed.), *John Witherspoon Comes to America: A Documentary Account Based Largely on New Materials* (Princeton, N. J., Princeton University Press, 1953).

[26] Margaret B. Deschamps, "Presbyterians and Southern Education," *Journal of the Presbyterian Historical Society,* XXXI (1953), 71-86.

ferson wrote his friend Thomas Cooper in 1822 that he feared the Presbyterians "aim, like the Jesuits, at engrossing the education of the country."[27]

Since the end of the colonial period the Scotch-Irish have been a dominant strain in American life. Their lean, ascetic faces peer from austere walls in capitols, courthouses, and colleges, and every gallery of America's great has a number of their portraits. Andrew Jackson, Woodrow Wilson, Andrew Mellon, and countless others of their stock have set one pattern of greatness—that of men, not to the manner born, who achieved their position through a combination of righteousness and industry.

John Filson belonged to these vigorous people who began their wandering in the narrow confines of Scotland and found themselves two centuries later on the boundless western lands of North America. In Ulster the family probably lived in Ballyeaston, near Ballyclare, in County Antrim. From there many Presbyterians with liberal tendencies and a scant respect for the Irish landlord system migrated to Pennsylvania around 1730.[28] With them must have been one John Filson, grandfather of the subject of this biography, for in 1729 his name appears for the first time on the list of taxables in Chester County.[29] From the tax lists it would appear that John Filson brought little of this world's wealth. We do know that he brought his family, the Presbyterian faith, and the momentum of independence. He settled permanently in Fallowfield Township and with the division of this township in 1743 found him-

27 Andrew Agate Lipscomb (ed.), *The Writings of Thomas Jefferson* (20 vols., Washington, Thomas Jefferson Memorial Association, 1903-1904), XV, 404-405.

28 From genealogical information in letters from Denis O'D. Hanna, Belfast, and Alexander Warnock Filson, Richmond, Surrey, dated September 18, 1953, and February 26, 1954, respectively. There were Filsons in the counties of Antrim and Down.

29 A list of taxables in Chester County, Pennsylvania; photostatic copy from the Cope Genealogical Collection in the Pennsylvania Historical Society, Philadelphia.

self in East Fallowfield. In the petitions addressed to the court for the division, the names of John *Filsell,* Robert Filson, Samiel Filsell, and William Filsell occur as inhabitants of the eastern part of the township.[30] About three years earlier, John Filson, William Hanna, Francis Boggs, James Blalock, and others had erected on the Strasburg Road a house of worship which was known as the "Doe Run Presbyterian Church." This congregation belonged to the New Side body of Presbyterians and was supplied with preachers from the Presbytery of New Castle until about 1747, when the Reverend Andrew Sterling became the regular pastor.[31]

John Filson, immigrant from Ulster, yeoman farmer, liberal Presbyterian, left his new home for an eternal one sometime between September 3, 1748, when his will was signed, and April 29, 1751, when it was ordered to record in the county court.[32] His estate was modest: a farm of two hundred acres, a new dwelling house, four cows, a heifer, and a "rising" horse. For his widow Jane he provided one half of the dwelling, a "sufficiency" of bread meal, and wood for one fire—cut and brought to her door—for the duration of her life. From this will we learn that John Filson had four children: Davison, John, William, and Margaret. That there were other children is shown by two deeds which name them as Robert, Samuel, Elizabeth, wife of George Liggett, and Jane, wife of James Patton.[33]

Davison Filson, father of John Filson of Kentucky, inherited his father's farm and lived on it until he died. At the time of his father's death he was unmarried; but on June 22, 1752, he and Eleanor Clarke said their nuptial vows in Old Swede's

[30] Excerpt from the Cope Collection in the Chester County Historical Society, West Chester, Pennsylvania. See also J. Smith Futhey and Gilbert Cope, *History of Chester County, Pennsylvania* (Philadelphia, L. H. Everts, 1881), 175-77.

[31] Futhey and Cope, 252.

[32] Will Book C, vol. 3, pp. 278-81, West Chester, Pennsylvania.

[33] Deed Book 2, p. 85, West Chester, Pennsylvania.

Church (Holy Trinity) Wilmington, Delaware.[34] Why Davison, the Presbyterian farmer from Chester County, should marry in the city parish of Holy Trinity is unknown. Eleanor may have lived in Wilmington; or more likely, on their wedding day Davison and Eleanor wanted something more cheerful than the spare Presbyterian meetinghouse on Doe Run. At all events, a Swedish parson, Israel Acrelius, solemnized the wedding and recorded it.

Davison Filson brought his bride home to the farm he had inherited, and there probably she died sometime before February 9, 1768; for on that date he married Agnes Boggs in the First Presbyterian Church in Philadelphia.[35] Davison barely lived to see the signing of the Declaration of Independence; his will was signed on August 2, 1776, and brought into court on August 23 of the same year.[36] He had increased his patrimony and had accumulated a personal estate valued at three hundred pounds, a respectable sum for a yeoman farmer on the Brandywine. His will, which would be the despair of a grammarian, is entirely satisfactory for the genealogist. In it Davison mentions his eight children: John, Robert, Ann, Eleanor, Moses, Jean, Elizabeth, and "the last one bourn and not naimed as yet." The pathos and poor spelling may cast gloom over remote descendants who examine the will; they should know that Rebecca[37]—for so the child was christened—survived. She married one of Scotia's blood, John Donaldson, and bore him six children. Thus the last seed of Davison fell on fertile soil.[38]

[34] Marriage record in Old Swede's (Holy Trinity) Church in Wilmington.

[35] *Pennsylvania Archives* (119 vols., Philadelphia, Harrisburg, 1852-1935), 2d ser., IX, 87.

[36] Will Book F, vol. 6, pp. 261-62, West Chester, Pennsylvania.

[37] Orphan's Court Record, vol. 8, p. 39, dated January 15, 1779, West Chester, Pennsylvania.

[38] For further genealogical information about the Filsons, see John Walton, "Notes on the Filson Family," *Filson Club History Quarterly,* XXVI (1952), 251-73.

These are the roots. This is the beginning of the Filson family in America. The humble and prosaic pattern of their lives has been repeated so often among the Scotch-Irish, and with slight variation, among the Puritans, that it has become the stereotype of early American ancestry outside the Cavalier country in Virginia. Yeoman farmers, Calvinistic, liberal, and independent, they served in the war that established American independence. Although the family was extremely small, comprising at the time of the War probably only the surviving sons and grandsons of the one immigrant, no fewer than twelve men by the name of Filson appear on the long rolls of the Revolution. During the course of the years since, the family has become neither numerous nor famous. An occasional clergyman, soldier, or journalist bearing the name has given the family a little luster now and then; but the only famous member was John—called John the Historian to distinguish him from his kinsmen by the same name and because he wrote a quaint little book about Kentucky, Daniel Boone, and the Indians.

Chapter 2 Early Life

THE CHILDHOOD and youth of John Filson are shrouded in obscurity. If the boy whom we do not know was the father of the man who became famous as the historian and cartographer of Kentucky, he must have been a restless, visionary youth, given to pretentious learning and annoying curiosity. All that is known—and probably all that will ever be known—about Filson from the day of his birth until he appeared in the new settlements of Kentucky is pieced together from several extremely fragmentary sources.

The date of John Filson's birth has long been a matter of speculation. Colonel Reuben Durrett made a bold guess that Filson was born in 1747;[1] although his evidence was derived from two sources, it was tenuous and misleading. Filson owned, and apparently treasured, a pocket-sized volume dismally entitled, *Admonitions from the Dead in Epistles to the Living: Addressed by Certain Spirits of Both Sexes to their Friends or Enemies on Earth, with a view either to condemn or justify their Conduct while alive; and to promote the Cause of Religion and Moral Virtue.*[2] On pages 17 and 47, the owner wrote his name, a fact which led Colonel Durrett to conjecture that this was the year of Filson's birth: "It has been the habit of some owners of books to write their names upon particular pages, the figures of which indicate the date of purchase, others the time of the owner's arriving at the age of twenty-one, etc. It was, possibly, the peculiarity of Filson to write his name on two separate pages, the figures of which, when joined together, would represent the year of his birth."[3]

Colonel Durrett believed that he found additional evidence to support his theory in the will of John Filson's grandfather. While it is true that John Filson the Elder does mention three grandsons—John and two Robert Filsons—in his will dated September 3, 1748, a careful reading of this will indicates beyond any presumption of doubt that Davison Filson, father of the historian, had no children at this time:

I give to my beloved Son Davison whome with my son John I constitute my executor of this my last Will and Testament, all and singular the Lands Messuages and Tenements, by him freely to be possessed and enjoyed by him, his heirs and assigns forever, being the place whereone I now dwell, containing by Estimation two hundred acres be it more or less, *But in Case he should* [die] *without issue,* then the said Messuage or Plantation shall be sold, and the value of it shall be Euqually divided to all my Children. Except my wife's previledge which shall still remain to her as aforesaid.[4]

Furthermore, Davison Filson married, surely for the first time, on June 22, 1752, a fact Colonel Durett did not know.[5] Not only is a date later than 1747 demanded by the will of John Filson the Elder and by the date of Davison's marriage, but there is also a family tradition that John Filson was born December 10, 1753.[6] Since this tradition is so consistent with

[1] Durrett, *John Filson,* 9.

[2] Copy now in the Filson Club, Louisville. The book was published by R. Baldwin, London, 1654.

[3] Durrett, 9.

[4] Will Book C, vol. 3, pp. 278-81, West Chester, Pennsylvania.

[5] Durrett, 8-9. He has a record of Davison's second marriage on February 9, 1768, to Agnes Boggs and speculated on the date of a previous marriage.

[6] Letter from Miss Margaret J. Marshall, Philadelphia, to the author. Miss Marshall is a descendant of Rebecca Filson Donaldson, sister of John Filson.

the evidence, it is assumed to be at least approximately correct for the birth date of Davison Filson's eldest son. As for the grandson John mentioned in the will of the first John Filson, he could have been the son of either William Filson or Samuel Filson, both of whom are known to have had sons named John.[7] The ingenious guess of Colonel Durrett, honestly made as a conjecture, has come to be accepted as true by many of Filson's biographers.[8]

There could have been little that was romantic about Filson's early life in the simple, rural, eighteenth century household in which he grew up. In Chester County's East Fallowfield Township, about two miles south of the present Strasburg Road, and somewhere between the West Branch of Brandywine Creek and Buck and Doe Run, stood the farmhouse of his father and grandfather,[9] where he was born and where he lived until he went to Wilmington to teach school.

So meager is the information about his early life that one simple story Filson told years later on the frontier has been handed down, not for its intrinsic interest, but rather because it provides the only glimpse we have into his childhood years. In 1784 Abram Hite, who was building a mill on Goose Creek, near Louisville, listened to Filson's pointless little anecdote and remembered it. Filson, enjoying the privileges of an eldest son, was often sent to the mill with a bag of corn thrown across the back of a horse. On one occasion, while combining a trip to the mill with some private explorations, he attempted to cross the Brandywine at an unfamiliar ford. Before reaching the opposite side of the stream, his horse plunged into water too deep to be waded and began swimming vigorously toward

7 See John Walton, "The Date of John Filson's Birth," *Bulletin of the Historical and Philosophical Society of Ohio,* XII (1954), 69-70.

8 Jillson, *Filson's Kentucke,* 139. Also, Samuel M. Wilson, "John Filson in Pennsylvania," *Filson Club History Quarterly,* XIII (1939), 185; and *Appleton's Cyclopedia of American Biography,* II, 457.

9 Wilson, 194.

the shore. As the water came over the back of the horse, the bag of corn was washed into the current, and Filson himself barely managed to stay astride. The next day younger brother Robert was sent to mill, and John was given the less agreeable task of hoeing corn.[10] This trite and insignificant tale, remembered out of all the tall stories of the frontier, is the one slender thread that connects us with the early life of John Filson. From it one can easily imagine a familiar pattern of boyhood life.

In addition to attending whatever common schools were available, Filson is reputed to have been a student at West Nottingham Academy in an adjoining county in Maryland,[11] where he studied Latin, Greek, French, and surveying. The records of the academy for the years Filson would have been in attendance have not been preserved,[12] but most of his biographers include Filson's attendance there as a fact.

Whether Filson attended the academy or not, he acquired a better education than most youths. Somewhere he had learned at least a smattering of Greek and Latin, and he knew enough French to advertise himself as a teacher of the subject in the culture-conscious frontier town of Lexington. Also, he was a surveyor of ability, and while this does not presuppose any advanced formal education, it was one of the things often expected of the rural scholar. Filson's literary style, although excessively florid, even for the time, is often vivid and attractive; and his allusions to events in the world of learning indicate strongly that he had read widely if indiscriminately, and he must have seemed quite erudite to the other farm boys in the neighborhood.

[10] Durrett, 10.

[11] West Nottingham Academy is located at Colora, Maryland, near the Pennsylvania line. Founded in 1744 by the Reverend Samuel Finley, who became president of Princeton in 1761, it is considered to be the oldest Presbyterian educational institution of any kind in existence on the North American continent.

[12] Letter dated October 6, 1953, from George William Dando, Alumni Representative, West Nottingham Academy, Colora, Maryland.

There are only vague references in secondary sources to Filson's activities immediately before and during the Revolution. He probably taught school and surveyed the lands of the thrifty farmers along the Brandywine, and later he is supposed to have opened a school in Wilmington.[13] Despite the efforts of industrious researchers, Filson's service in the army, if indeed he served at all, has never been substantiated. It is possible that he served either in the Continental Army[14] or in the militia of Pennsylvania or Delaware. The records of the Pennsylvania militia show that a John Fillson, Senior, and a John Fillson, Junior, were in the Seventh Class, Eighth Battalion, Chester County Militia, during the years 1780 and 1781.[15] The designations "Senior" and "Junior" do not necessarily refer to father and son but were often used to distinguish between two men of the same name. Since there were at least two John Filsons in Pennsylvania, both first cousins of the historian, who were old enough to have served in the militia during these years,[16] this proves nothing so far as our problem is concerned. There is also a record of the service of a John Filson as an ensign in Montgomery's Pennsylvania Battalion of the Flying Camp; he was taken prisoner at Fort Washington, November 16, 1776, but he is not otherwise identified.[17]

[13] Henry C. Conrad, *History of the State of Delaware* (3 vols., Wilmington, Author, 1908), I, 313-14. Filson is known to have taught in Wilmington in 1785. See Chapter VII.

[14] Although there is no record of Filson's service in the Adjutant General's Office in Washington, D. C., or in the National Archives.

[15] *Pennsylvania Archives,* 5th ser., V, 824, 835, 841.

[16] John Filson, uncle of the historian, died in 1750. However, both Samuel Filson and William Filson, also uncles of the historian, had sons named John, both of whom were probably born early enough to have served in the Revolution. It is also possible that another uncle, Robert Filson, had a son John. See Walton, "Notes on the Filson Family."

[17] Francis B. Heitman, *Historical Register of the Officers of the Continental Army* (Washington, Rare Book Shop Publishing Company, 1914), 226. Heitman also lists a Robert Filson, first lieutenant of Montgomery's Pennsylvania Battalion of the Flying Camp, who was taken prisoner at Fort Washington on the same day. The surrender at Fort Washington is mentioned in one of Washington's letters to General Lee dated November 16, 1776. Washington was then in

Finding no official record of Filson's service, Colonel Durrett thought that he might have stayed out of service because of his occupation, but this statement is only a surmise.[18] The Delaware historians have preserved a tradition that Filson served in the war and was wounded in the right arm:

James Filson taught school in Wilmington before the Revolution. He returned from the Army with no injury save a slight wound in the right arm. He again opened his school in 1785 [?] and continued it for two years. His wounded arm prevented him from 'thrashing the boys' as he thought they deserved; so he abandoned his profession, went to Kentucky, and was one of the early adventurers there with Daniel Boone.[19]

He [Filson] served in the War of the Revolution, and was wounded in the right arm. Soon after the war he again opened the school, and continued it for a few years. The complaint was made that owing to the wound in his arm he was unable to thrash the boys, and this led him to abandon the profession of teaching; so leaving Wilmington, he went to Kentucky, and with Daniel Boone was one of the adventurers there.[20]

John Filson is listed in the archives of the state as one of the Delawareans who served in the war,[21] but his name appears in a supplemental list and was taken from Conrad's history. Unfortunately, none of the Delaware historians give the source of their information.

If Filson did not serve in the Revolutionary War—and it appears somewhat doubtful that he did—one may well ask why.

---

headquarters at Hackensack (William S. Baker, *Itinerary of General Washington 1775-1783* [Philadelphia, J. P. Lippincott Company, 1892], 56). Montgomery's Flying Camp was a Chester County battalion (*Pennsylvania Archives,* 2d ser., XIV, 757). However, there appears to be no way of determining whether this John Filson was the subject of this biography or one of his cousins. No information is available in either the Division of Public Records, Harrisburg, or in the Historical Society of Pennsylvania, Philadelphia.

18 Durrett, 12.

19 J. Thomas Scharf, *History of Delaware* (2 vols., Philadelphia, L. J. Richards & Co., 1888), II, 684. Author's italics.

20 Conrad, I, 313-14.

21 *Delaware Archives* (5 vols., Wilmington, 1911-1916), II, 1011.

Most of his kinsmen were in either the Pennsylvania Line or the militia. He was unmarried and of military age. And it is hardly conceivable that he was a pacificist or a Tory. Some clue may be found in the will of his father written in August, 1776, in which Davison Filson names his son Robert and his "beloved frend" William Grant as executors of his small estate, notwithstanding the fact that John was the eldest son and doubtless the best educated member of the family. We may infer from this one of two things: either John was not in the good graces of his father at the time, or he was living away from Chester County. The latter seems the more probable as John inherited by this will two cows and the release from half of the debt he owed his father for land. Furthermore, with his brother Robert he was given the responsibility of educating his two young sisters, Jean and Elizabeth. If John was teaching school in Wilmington, his father would have good reason for leaving the settlement of his estate in the hands of his second son and of a neighboring farmer. Since Davison left five children under age—Ann, Eleanor, Jean, Moses, Elizabeth, and the newborn Rebecca—John, being unmarried, might have returned home to help care for the family. Robert was married, with at least one child of his own by this time.[22] Thus Colonel Durrett's guess that John Filson spent the bitter years of the war as a schoolmaster in Chester County is plausible.

These few facts and cautious surmises are all that are known or can be reasonably conjectured about the man who was to enjoy a brief renown a few years hence. As the first historian of Kentucky, the biographer of Boone, and a cartographer of extraordinary ability, he achieved fame in Europe as well as in America. The interest that he aroused, however, was in his subjects rather than in himself, and no one took the pains to set down the facts about the author's life or his antecedents. After his disappearance, the settlement of the western country

[22] See Walton, "Notes on the Filson Family," 254.

rolled on, and in its course the first chronicler of the frontier was forgotten for almost a hundred years.

Before we leave the vain search for information about the young Filson, it may add to our scant knowledge to examine the only likeness extant, although it will do little to enhance our opinion of him. On the flyleaf of his well-worn little volume, *Admonitions from the Dead in Epistles to the Living,* someone attempted to draw a man's picture. Beneath it is the signature of John Filson. This miniature, obviously the work of an amateur, is sketched in pencil and toned with an ink wash. So sepulchral is the aspect of the man that he could well be one of the spirits whose admonitions are included in the book. The face is neither handsome nor prepossessing, and the large, mournful eyes bespeak a hopeless despair. Incongruously, the man is a dandy. Stiffly bound up in a high-buttoned vest, a cravat, and a coat in the style of pre-Revolutionary France, this melodramatic little man bears slight resemblance to the stereotype of the American frontiersman. If Filson's appearance and his taste in literature are accurately portrayed in this likeness and in the book he treasured, he obviously was steeped in the romantic spirit of the late eighteenth century. The weird "epistles" of Madame Maintenon to Voltaire, of Archbishop Tillotson to another bishop, and of the Duke of Buckingham to his mother all appear to have been read and reread. In Kentucky these ghostly letters must have lost some of their fascination as Filson listened to the tales of Indian horrors told by living heroes.

Chapter 3 Kentucke

IF JOHN FILSON passed through the harsh, tense years of the Revolution in the comparative peace of a colonial schoolroom within earshot of the fierce and obstinate Battle of the Brandywine, he was destined to spend the remaining few years of his life in the adventures, the hazards, and the tragedies of the frontier. Kentucky, the lodestone that attracted so many of the victorious American soldiers, drew him also across the Appalachian barrier. At least three times he returned to the settled life in old Chester County, but each time the memory of stirring events along the Ohio was strong enough to send him back through the forest trails to Kentucky.

Daniel Boone had gone from the Yadkin to Kentucky in 1769, and James Harrod from the Monongahela in 1774. Both had established permanent settlements before the war with the British began, and they held on tenaciously during the Indian invasions from north of the Ohio.[1] While the Indian depredations continued and the eastern colonists were engaged in the struggle for independence, migration to the western lands was desultory; but as soon as the British were defeated and the Indians discouraged in their hopes of driving the white men from the hunting grounds, the settlement began in earnest. The energies of the colonists were far from exhausted by the war they had just won; and whatever apathy they showed to the problems of government, they were stimulated to exploit the advantages of an unsettled continent. With British rule out of the way there were unmeasured acres of land to be taken by those who had the energy and the courage. These two qualities the colonists had above all others.

Kentucky had already become a promised land. Beyond the soft contours of the Blue Ridge were the harsher outlines of the Alleghenies; and beyond both the long chain of the Cumberlands, range upon range, until the mountains ended abruptly in the rich, uninhabited meadows that stretched endlessly westward. For upwards of three decades, tales of the long hunters who had been across the mountains—the leather-stockinged men—had described a land of myth and legend, pierced by mammoth caves and laced with silent, shining rivers, a land incredibly fertile and entirely uninhabited by the Indians.[2] The period of exploration was coming to an end; the time of settlement had come. All the pent-up eagerness to migrate to such a region now burst forth; and at the war's end the mighty procession to Kentucky was under way, the beginning of one of the most extensive migrations in human history.[3] From practically all the eastern colonies—Massachusetts, Rhode Island, New York, New Jersey, Pennsylvania, Delaware, Maryland, Virginia, and the Carolinas[4]—and from along the north Atlantic—London, Dublin, Stockholm, and Bordeaux[5]—came

1 One of the best secondary sources for the early history of Kentucky is R. S. Cotterill, *History of Pioneer Kentucky* (Cincinnati, Johnson & Hardin, 1917). See also the extensive bibliography on the early history of the state in Thomas D. Clark, *A History of Kentucky* (New York, Prentice-Hall, 1937), 627-36.

2 J. Stoddard Johnston, *First Explorations of Kentucky* (Filson Club *Publications,* no. 13, Louisville, 1898). See particularly "Colonel Christopher Gist's Journal of a Tour Through Ohio and Kentucky in 1751," pp. 101-85.

3 Cotterill, 150-76.

4 See "Place of Residence" of the Grantees of Deeds in Willard Rouse Jillson, *Old Kentucky Entries and Deeds* (Filson Club *Publications,* no. 34, Louisville, 1926), 393-464. Also, Evarts Boutell Greene, *The Revolutionary Generation* (New York, Macmillan Company, 1943), 401-23.

5 Willard Rouse Jillson, *Pioneer Kentucky* (Frankfort, State Journal Company, 1934), 16.

adventurers, hunters, farmers, and traders, all lured by the prospect of being the first men in a new civilization. Among the many who came was the small, curious schoolmaster from Chester County.

The exact date of John Filson's first arrival in Kentucky is unknown. Colonel Durrett says that he came over the mountains to Pittsburgh, down the Ohio River to Limestone, an important point of entry for the new settlers, and from there through the forests to Lexington.[6] Following this route Filson as a surveyor and a man with an eye to the future development of the West must have made calculations on distances, possibilities for navigation, and the fertility of the soil. In floating southward down the Ohio he passed the mouth of the Kanawha, a stream that might be navigable to a point nearer to the eastern ports than Pittsburgh was; and in traveling overland to Lexington he could not help noting the abundance and the lushness of the cane on the fine lands he passed through. This journey must have been made in the early fall of 1783, although Ranck in his history of Lexington has Filson teaching school in that city in 1782: "Lexington station gained another school-teacher this year [1782], in the person of John Filson, the author, in 1784, of the first history ever written of Kentucky."[7] However, the first contemporary to report that Filson was in the land was Colonel William Sudduth, who had come from Fauquier County, Virginia, in October, 1783, and had spent the winter, from December 11 to June 1, at Strode's Station.[8] "Filson, I think, was at Strode's Station while I was

[6] Durrett, *John Filson,* 13.

[7] George W. Ranck, *History of Lexington, Kentucky* (Cincinnati, R. Clarke & Co., 1872), 96.

"John Filson, the surveyor, adventurer, and first historian of Kentucky, as well as teacher, established a seminary in Lexington in or before 1784." Alvin Fayette Lewis, *History of Higher Education in Kentucky* (Washington, Government Printing Office, 1899), 12. The author gives no authority for his statement.

[8] "Strode settled across the river from Boonesborough in what was later Clarke County." Cotterill, 152.

there; was making out a map, and surveying some on the Ohio at the time. Understood that he measured the Ohio from Pittsburgh to the Falls."[9]

If Filson had already surveyed the Ohio as far west as the Falls, he must have come to Kentucky sometime before Sudduth knew of him at Strode's Station. The evidence is fairly conclusive that Filson came to Kentucky between September 12, 1783, and December 19 of the same year. On the earlier date he executed a note to one Joseph Speer of Chester County for eleven pounds, nine shillings, two pence in the gold or silver currency of Pennsylvania. This note was paid by his brother Robert Filson in Chester County on May 1, 1784, to Joseph Speer.[10] If Filson was in Chester County on the day he gave the note to Speer,[11] it is necessary to assume that he started for Kentucky soon afterward. The journey from Pennsylvania to Kentucky would require at least a month, so that the very earliest he could have arrived was the middle of October. And we know that he was there at least some days or weeks before December 19, for on that date and the day following, he claimed three large tracts of land.

John Filson assee of Clem Moore enteres 5000 acres of land on part of a Treasury Warrant No. 19606 lying on the waters of Ohio and about 10 or 11 miles eastward of the big Bone Lick. Beginning at the north-eastward corner of an entry made in the name of Benjamin Netherland for 7000 acres and running north with the lines of older entries 1200 poles and also from said Beginning south 20 west with Netherlands line to the line of an entry made in the

9 Kentucky Papers, Draper Collection of Manuscripts, State Historical Society, Madison, Wisconsin, 12CC61-64; microfilm copy in the Princeton University Library.

10 Original note in the Clarke Collection, Historical and Philosophical Society of Ohio, Cincinnati.

11 There is no evidence that Joseph Speer was ever in Kentucky. He was taxed in Chester County for the years 1779, 1781, and 1785 (the tax lists for the intervening years are not available), and he certainly was there on May 1, 1784, when Robert Filson paid the note. *Pennsylvania Archives,* 3d ser., XII, 187, 461, 582, 636, 718, 748.

name of James Lyle, jr. for 500 acres, thence South, etc. Decr. 19th, 1783.

John Filson assee & c enteres 4922 acres of land on the ballance of a Treasury Warrant No 19606 lying about 5 or 6 miles from the Ohio River, Beginning at the most West corner of an entry made in the name of Humphrey Marshall for 3,000 acres and running from, thence and with the line of said entry South 40 East and continuing the Same course 800 poles, etc. Decr. 19th 1783.

John Filson, assee, Enteres 2446½ acres on two Treasury Warrants one belonging to John Boyd No. 14,934, the other assigned to John Filson No. 10,758 as tenant adjoining on the northerly side with said Boyd about 10 or 11 miles south of Ohio River, beginning at the most westerly corner of an entry of John Filson's, thence by the line of said Entry of 4922 acres south 40 East and continuing the same course 625 poles, etc. Decr. 20, 1783.[12]

These entries, which were made so hurriedly after Filson arrived in Kentucky, furnish ample evidence of why he came. Kentucky, then still a part of Virginia, by May, 1780, had been divided into three counties—Lincoln, Fayette, and Jefferson—in order to provide for the better administration of justice.[13] One of the problems that was beginning to plague the officials in the mother state was that of land titles. In addition to the lands Virginia granted her soldiers and those already claimed by the earliest settlers, there were still thousands of acres available in Kentucky.[14] Not being a proprietary colony, Virginia had earlier established a policy of attracting settlers to her western lands by cheap land prices and low taxes.[15] Successive

[12] Register of Colonel Thomas Marshall, surveyor of Fayette County, Book 3, pp. 101, 102, 106. Copied from Durrett, 114-15. See also Jillson, *Old Kentucky Entries and Deeds,* 98.

[13] William Waller Hening, *The Statutes at Large, Being a Collection of All the Laws of Virginia* (13 vols., Richmond, Samuel Pleasants, etc., 1810-1823), X, 315-17. See also Morgan Poitiaux Robinson, *Virginia Counties: Those Resulting from Virginia Legislation* (Virginia State Library *Bulletins,* no. 9, Richmond, 1916), 140, 145, 146.

[14] Jillson, *Old Kentucky Entries and Deeds,* 1-9.

[15] Brydon,*Virginia's Mother Church,* 154. See also Thomas Perkins Abernethy, *Western Lands and the American Revolution* (New York, D. Appleton-Century Company, 1937).

waves of migration were beginning to complicate the matter of titles, so that by 1777 the General Assembly had made some effort to clarify the status of settlers "upon unappropriated lands, to which there was no prior just claim."[16] Two years later the Assembly passed the land law of 1779, which provided that future titles to Kentucky lands could be obtained only through treasury warrants.[17] The price of the land was fixed at forty pounds for one hundred acres; the quantity of land purchased was to be surveyed by an official surveyor in Kentucky, and the plat and certificate returned to Richmond; and a deed sent from there to the warrantee.

It was under this land law—with the exception that in 1781 a deputy land register had been provided for in Kentucky so that persons who took the land would not have to travel to Richmond to obtain their title papers[18]—that Filson claimed his land. Since there is no evidence that Filson had received a military warrant,[19] we must assume that he paid a total of something like 5,000 pounds in Virginia currency for his 12,000 or more acres. Virginia currency had depreciated so rapidly during the war that this sum was not at all what it appears to be. Some idea of the extent may be obtained from some contemporary records of prices in Virginia. In 1780 a student at the College of William and Mary wrote his uncle that he would find it difficult to return to college the next year because of the depreciation of the value of Virginia money.[20] A year later wagon hire was reported to cost from sixteen to twenty pounds

[16] Hening, IX, 355. [17] *Ibid.*, X, 35-50, 50-66. [18] *Ibid.*, 445.

[19] Despite the inference in the account of Filson in *Dictionary of American Biography*, VI, 382, that his land warrants in Kentucky indicate military service; and Marshall W. Fishwick's statement that they were military warrants, in "Daniel Boone and the Pattern of the Western Hero," 124. The records of the Virginia land grants do not contain the name of John Filson. In a letter dated February 2, 1955, William J. Van Schreeven, state archivist for Virginia, wrote, "If he [Filson] acquired land himself by purchase from another, such an acquisition would not be recorded as a land grant, but rather as a deed."

[20] Letters from John Brown to William Preston, dated January 26, 1780, *William and Mary Quarterly*, 1st ser., IX (1900-1901), 75.

per day and corn to cost twenty-five pounds per barrel. The rate of exchange of Virginia currency with the "new Congress dollars" was only half as favorable as that of Pennsylvania and New Jersey currency, and even at that rate, speculators alone seemed interested.[21] On the basis of these facts, Colonel Durrett's statement that by 1783 Virginia paper currency was worth only a thousand to one of silver may not be an exaggeration.[22] At all events, the sum of 5,000 pounds in Virginia currency was not beyond the financial ability of a thirty-year-old schoolteacher.

Land grabbing was an eminently respectable pursuit among the settlers, and since the land was not immediately productive, a man might reasonably be expected to follow a trade until his fortunes were realized. The earliest references to Filson have him surveying and teaching school: the first, one of the most practical and respected vocations on the frontier; and the second, not without at least some respectability in a town like Lexington. Filson, however, immediately set about a third, and most extraordinary, activity—he began writing a book.

Although it must have seemed a strange vagary to the Kentuckians, there are several reasons why Filson should want to write a book. He was an impressionable young man and was excited by what he saw happening: people were arriving daily and their number was increasing; optimism was rampant; and the land really was fertile beyond any he had ever seen. He also shrewdly foresaw that increased immigration to the state would enhance land values and thereby increase the worth of his own extensive holdings. While it would be unjust to impute mercenary motives alone to the author of the first book about Kentucky, the internal evidence is conclusive that it is

[21] *Calendar of Virginia State Papers* (11 vols., Richmond, 1875-1893), I, 509, 516. For the background of Virginia currency, see William Zebina Ripley, *The Financial History of Virginia, 1609-1776* (Columbia College *Studies in History, Economics, and Public Law,* no. 4, New York, 1893).

[22] Durrett, 14.

a piece of promotional literature. Filson's book did speed the settlement of the state, but in the uncertainty and complexity of human affairs the author realized nothing from it. Before the land had acquired any great value, Filson had vanished; and it is extremely doubtful that his titles were valid anyway. The land law of 1779 was cumbersome, and many of the warrants issued were later invalidated.

For his literary purpose, Filson arrived in Kentucky at an opportune time. The first year that he was there was a comparatively peaceful one; the Indian Wars had subsided after the frightful carnage of the battle with the Wyandots at the Lower Blue Licks in August of the year before.[23] A deep impression had been made on the minds of the Kentuckians by the enormity of their losses and the magnitude of the pioneer's task. During the respite from the depredations of the Indians, tales of the events of the past few years were repeated and magnified. The legends of Kentucky were in the making. The Kentuckians were in the mood to talk and Filson was an indefatigable inquirer. As he traveled from station to station, surveying and questioning, he acquired a reputation for annoying persistence. In the traditions of the frontiersmen it has been handed down that he could ask more questions than everybody and answer fewer than anybody.[24] The Indian fighters were probably quite willing to reminisce, but they must have chafed under Filson's demands for precise information.

The information in Filson's book was obtained from the best available sources—Daniel Boone, Levi Todd, James Harrod, Christopher Greenup, John Cowan, and William Kennedy.[25] These men knew Kentucky. Boone, who knew and loved Kentucky as no other man, had been willing to talk to Filson about his adventures and had thereby assured his immortality in the

[23] Cotterill, 177-95. [24] Durrett, 16.

[25] Filson gave credit to these men for having provided some of the information for his map (see inscriptions on map). Doubtless much of the same information was used in his description of Kentucky.

legends of America.[26] Levi Todd, at whose house near Lexington Filson did most of his writing, was one of the best educated and most reliable of the pioneers.[27] Among the others, James Harrod, who had come to Kentucky in 1774, was an upright man and almost the equal of Boone as a woodsman. He, like Filson, was to disappear mysteriously, probably while looking for a mythical silver mine.[28] These men had explored the creeks and rivers, noted the fauna and the flora, and appraised the fertility and wealth of the land in which they had chosen to live. Filson owed the reliability of the vast amount of information he collected in so short a time to the experience and co-operation of these pioneers who had come to Kentucky before him. The accuracy of the map, on which the author had less opportunity to speculate and improvise than he did in his book, indicates the competence and the veracity of these men.

This first visit of Filson to Kentucky was something of a tour de force. In less than a year he had entered a vast tract of real estate in his name, taught school, written a book, and drawn an excellent map, all in a land that was strange to him. Since there were no printing presses or engravers west of the Alleghenies, Filson, with characteristic haste, left Kentucky for Wilmington and Philadelphia in the early summer of 1784, carrying his manuscripts with him.[29] However, his contact with Kentucky had just begun; in the four years that he had to live, the stimulus of the vast new West kept him rushing feverishly about, attempting much and failing often, until the fates that brooded over America's frontiers made an end to his rather pathetic endeavors.

[26] See Chapter V. [27] Durrett, 22.

[28] *Ibid.* See also Lewis Collins, *History of Kentucky* (2 vols., Covington, Collins & Co., 1874), II, 414-15. Also, Clark, 43-44; and Kathryn Harrod Mason, *James Harrod of Kentucky* (Baton Rouge, Louisiana State University Press, 1951), 225-36.

[29] Filson was in Kentucky as late as May 12, for on that date Boone, Todd, and Harrod endorsed his book.

Chapter 4 The Book

PHILADELPHIANS who read the *Pennsylvania Packet and Daily Advertiser* on October 22, 1784, saw this notice:

> This Day is Published
> (Price one Dollar and a Half)
>
> And to be sold by Dunlap & Claypoole, Philadelphia, and James Adams, in Wilmington.
>
> *The Discovery, Settlement, and present State of Kentucky,* and an Essay towards the *Topography* and *Natural History of* that *important Country:* To which is added, *an Appendix* Containing, 1. The Adventures of Colonel Daniel Boon, one of the first settlers; comprehending every important occurence in the political history of that district; 2. The Minutes of the Piankashaw Council, held at Post St. Vincent's, April 15, 1784; 3. An Account of the Indian Nations inhabiting within the limits of the United States, their manners and customs, and reflections on their origin; 4. The stages and distances between Philadelphia and the falls of the Ohio, by land; from Pittsburg down the Ohio and Mississippi Rivers, to the Mexican Gulph. The whole illustrated by a new and accurate map of Kentucke, and part of the Indiana Territory adjoining; drawn from actual observations, by John Filson.[1]

The advertisement concludes with a reminder to "the gentlemen who have favored this work with their subscriptions" that they may obtain copies at Major Hareer's (Harper's) tavern in Chester, Mr. Edge's store in Downing's-town, or Mr. Jordon's tavern in Lancaster.

Despite its long title—a style which had considerable vogue among bookmakers at the time—this pretentious little volume contained only 118 pages. It was printed by James Adams, an Ulsterman and the first printer in Delaware, who had set up his own printing establishment in Wilmington about 1760;[2] and the accompanying map was engraved by Henry Pursell and printed by Ternon Rook, both of Philadelphia.

This Kentucky miscellany, consisting of an essay on the geography of the region, the Boone narrative, an account of the Indians, and a table of distances, bore striking similarities in structure to Jefferson's *Notes on the State of Virginia.* Both begin with a description of the boundaries of their respective states, followed by chapters on rivers, climate, produce, Indians, trade, population, and natural wonders.[3] Jefferson's work, written in 1781, was published first in 1785 in Paris;[4] however, manuscript copies of these *Notes* were in circulation during the interval,[5] and a copy Filson might have seen was in the hands of Charles Thomson, Secretary of the Continental Congress in Philadelphia. But there is another and perhaps more plausible hypothesis to acount for the similarity: Jefferson's *Notes* were written in response to and organized around twenty-three queries addressed to several Americans by the Marquis François de Barbé-Marbois, Secretary of the French legation

[1] Subsequent issues of the newspaper—October 27, November 10, 17, 22, 25, December 1, of the same year—carried the same advertisement with minor changes in spelling and punctuation. The newspaper was printed and sold on the south side of Market Street, the third house east of Second Street. See Samuel M. Wilson, "John Filson in Pennsylvania," 199-200.

[2] Dorothy Lawson Hawkins, "James Adams, the First Printer of Delaware," *Papers of the Bibliographical Society of America,* XXVIII (1934), 29.

[3] Jefferson's work is considerably longer, with separate chapters on colleges, religion, manners, Tories, and other topics which were not applicable to Kentucky or which Filson included in other chapters. See Thomas Jefferson, *Notes on the State of Virginia* (8th ed., Boston, Thomas & Andrews, 1801).

[4] For an excellent account of the writing and publication of Jefferson's *Notes on the State of Virginia,* see Marie Kimball, *Jefferson—War and Peace, 1776-1784* (New York, Coward-McCann, Inc., 1947), 259-305.

[5] *Ibid.,* 273.

in Philadelphia, for information about their respective states.[6] It is quite possible that Filson had seen a copy of these queries and organized his essay on Kentucky around them.[7] The fact that his *Kentucke* was published in France in 1785 lends some support to this theory.

Jefferson's *Notes on Virginia* was not the only precedent Filson had for supplying Europeans with information about America. As early as 1588 one Thomas Harriot had published *A Briefe and True Report of the New Found Land of Virginia, of Its Commodities, and of the Nature and Manner of the Natural Inhabitants,* a glowing account designed to foster colonization. And there were many other similar works published between that date and 1784 in England, France, and Germany.[8] But Filson's was the first book on Kentucky, and as such it is one of the most important documents in the history of the western development of the United States.[9]

In the Preface, Filson gives a forthright, if somewhat naive, reason for writing the book: "When I visited Kentucke, I found it so far to exceed my expectations, although great, that I concluded it was a pity; that the world had not adequate information of it."[10] And with a protestation that may appear suspicious in its earnestness, he continues: "and therefore, incredible as it may appear to some, I must declare, that this performance is not published from lucrative motives, but solely to inform the world of the happy climate, and plentiful soil of this favoured region."

6 *Ibid.,* 275. The only other reply to Marbois' queries that seems to have survived is that of Major General John Sullivan of New Hampshire, which is now in the Huntington Library.

7 It is known that Thomas McKean of Delaware had received a set, and there were probably others in the vicinity of Philadelphia. Dumas Malone, *Jefferson the Virginian* (Boston, Little, Brown and Company, 1948), 375, n. 5.

8 See Kimball, 265-67.

9 Marshall B. Davidson, *Life in America* (2 vols., Boston, Houghton Mifflin Company, 1951), I, 161-65.

10 Filson's *Kentucke,* 5.

THE

DISCOVERY, SETTLEMENT

And present State of

KENTUCKE:

AND

An ESSAY towards the TOPOGRAPHY, and NATURAL HISTORY of that important Country:

To which is added,

An APPENDIX,

CONTAINING,

I. The ADVENTURES of Col. *Daniel Boon*, one of the first Settlers, comprehending every important Occurrence in the political History of that Province.

II The MINUTES of the *Piankashaw* council, held at *Post St. Vincents*, *April* 15, 1784.

III. An ACCOUNT of the *Indian* Nations inhabiting within the Limits of the Thirteen United States, their Manners and Customs, and Reflections on their Origin.

IV. The STAGES and DISTANCES between *Philadelphia* and the Falls of the *Ohio*; from *Pittsburg* to *Pensacola* and several other Places. —The Whole illustrated by a new and accurate MAP of *Kentucke* and the Country adjoining, drawn from actual Surveys.

By *JOHN FILSON*.

Wilmington, Printed by JAMES ADAMS, 1784.

Title page of the first edition of John Filson's *Kentucke*
Courtesy of J. Winston Coleman, Jr., Lexington

It is very doubtful, in fact, that Filson expected to profit directly from the sale of the book; but he certainly hoped that it would bring settlers to Kentucky and thereby increase the value of his lands. Fearful of being accused of exaggeration, he called twice upon the three best-informed Kentuckians—Daniel Boone, Levi Todd, and James Harrod—to witness to the accuracy of his account. First, he attached an endorsement of his work, signed by these three men, in which they recommend the book and the map "as exceeding good performances, containing as accurate a description of our country as we think can possibly be given." That Filson relied heavily on this endorsement not only for the sale of the book, but also for the prestige of authority is clearly indicated by the fact that he carefully called attention to their recommendation in the Preface.[11]

The promised-land motif runs throughout the essay—a land extraordinarily beautiful, amazingly fertile, and singularly free from the pestilences of nature. One James McBride, said by Filson to be the first white man to have visited Kentucky,[12] returned with the report that he had discovered the best tract of land in North America and probably in the world! Filson described it as "the most extraordinary country that the sun enlightens with his celestial beams,"[13] where there grew cane twelve feet high and a variety of flowering trees; where serpents were not numerous and swamps rare.

Filson attempted to bolster his superlatives with sober statistics that could be understood by the farmers along the eastern seaboard, although placing some strain on their credulity. Reliable persons had reported to Filson while he was in Kentucky

[11] *Ibid.,* 6.

[12] An error. See Cotterill, *History of Pioneer Kentucky,* 42-48.

[13] *Kentucke,* 21. In a modern atlas central Kentucky is described as follows: "Bluegrass thrives on phosphorous content of limestone bedrock, which is six times as great as most fertile soils, provides such nutritious grazing that yearling colts in Kentucky reach mature size at 18 to 20 months." Herbert Bayer, *World Geographic Atlas* (Chicago, Container Corporation of America, 1953), 114.

that their land produced more than a hundred bushels of good corn to the acre, and that the first-rate land was too rich for wheat until it had been "reduced" by four or five years of cultivation.[14]

For those to whom the prospect of tilling the soil, however fertile, was no inducement, Filson reported that game was abundant. The quadrupeds included buffalo, deer, beaver, rabbits, squirrels, and opossums; in the streams were mullet, perch, suckers, sunfish, salmon—up to thirtyweight—and catfish, exceeding one hundredweight; and among the "plumy" tribe he had seen flocks of turkeys, innumerable pheasants, and an occasional ivory-billed woodcock.[15]

The white inhabitants—some thirty thousand souls—were described as polite, humane, hospitable, and "very complaisant."[16] Having migrated from many different parts, they represented a diversity of manners and customs. Schools were already being formed, and a college had been established by an act of the Virginia Assembly.[17] Although only Anabaptists and the Presbyterians had organized congregations, several other sects had numerous adherents.

But Kentucky was not only a land with complacent inhabitants and established institutions; it was also a place of curiosities, legends, and mysteries. Filson told of mammoth caves, ancient sepulchers filled with human skeletons, and enormous remains of prehistoric monsters.

At a salt spring, near Ohio river, very large bones are found, far surpassing the size of any species of animals now in America. The head appears to have been about three feet long, the ribs seven, and the thigh bones about four; one of which is reposited in the library in Philadelphia, and said to weigh seventy-eight pounds. The tusks are about a foot in length, the grinders about five inches

14 *Kentucke,* 24-25. 15 *Ibid.,* 26. 16 *Ibid.,* 29.

17 Transylvania University, created by an act of the Virginia General Assembly, at the May session, 1780. See Robert Peter, *Transylvania University* (Filson Club *Publications,* no. 11, Louisville, 1896), 17-20.

square, and eight inches long. These bones have equally excited the amazement of the ignorant, and attracted the attention of the philosopher.[18]

These bones must have intrigued Filson, as he devoted three pages to their description. Near the end he allowed himself a few sentences to reflect on the circumstances of the disappearance of so mighty a species: "Can then so great a link have perished from the chain of nature? Happy we that it has. How formidable an enemy to the human species, an animal as large as the elephant, the tyrant of the forests, perhaps the devourer of man!"[19] Actually these bones belonged to large extinct herbivorous pachyderms, a fact that was known at the time. George Rogers Clark had written to Jefferson from Louisville, "the animal had no foreteeth that I could ever discover and by no means Carnivorious as many suppose."[20] If Filson knew this, he nevertheless did not let it deprive him of an impressive climax.

After several pages hyperbole and mystery gave way to matter-of-fact information about how rights to the land may be obtained. Clearly and concisely the author instructed his readers how to proceed in making the original entry, surveying the claim, and obtaining the patent. And in order to dispel a rumor that Virginia might not have a valid claim to Kentucky, he cited the Treaty of Paris, 1763, which fixed the western boundary of the state as the Ohio River: "Therefore we conclude, that the right of Virginia to Kentucke is as permanent as the independence of America."[21]

With extraordinary vision he foresaw the advantages of the Ohio and Mississippi waterways as trade routes, and he gave a remarkably accurate description of their courses, obviously

[18] *Kentucke,* 33-34. [19] *Ibid.,* 36.

[20] George Rogers Clark in a letter dated February 20, 1782. Julian P. Boyd and others (eds.), *The Papers of Thomas Jefferson* (10 vols. to date, Princeton, N. J., Princeton University Press, 1950-), VI, 159.

[21] *Kentucke,* 38.

taken in part from Charlevoix.[22] He also foresaw the necessity of the port of New Orleans coming into the possession of the United States, an event some twenty years in the future.

In his description of the Indian tribes—twenty-eight nations in all living east of the Mississippi and numbering some twenty thousand—Filson revealed the characteristic attitude of the frontiersman toward the natives. He summarily dismissed the question of their origin by accepting the hypothesis that they came across the narrow strait that divides America from Asia, and he concluded that no further inquiry would ever be made into the matter. Any theorizing about their origin he described as "speculations of curious idleness" indulged in by people in the Old World.[23] To Filson as to most early Americans the Indian was a savage, and not the beautiful savage so dear to the romantic imaginations of the Europeans. If there was anything of the Calvinist left in Filson, he could hardly behold these pagans with any degree of favor. Moreover, the Indians were an ever-present menace, a threat to life and property. They had interfered with the white man's destiny, which was to occupy the choice lands of the earth and to establish his institutions to the ends of it.[24] However, Filson did not fail to note the virtues of the red men—virtues that all frontiersmen could recognize and respect. The Indians were strong and swift, hardy and stoical, and generally free from physical deformities. Some secret admiration for them must still remain in the American soul. As a sort of recompense we have kept their names on the rivers, forests, and mountains that they once knew. And perhaps the American nomadism

22 Pierre de Charlevoix, *Histoire et description generale de la Nouvelle France* (3 vols., Paris, Nyon fils, 1744).

23 *Kentucke,* 91.

24 Even Benjamin Franklin wrote of the "design of Providence to extirpate those savages in order to make room for the cultivators of the earth." *Autobiography* (New York, P. F. Collier & Sons, 1909), 121. For Franklin's and other Americans' complex attitudes toward the natives of North America, see Roy Harvey Pearce, *The Savages of America,* (Baltimore, Johns Hopkins Press, 1953).

may reveal an Indian component hidden in the American spirit.[25]

If Filson's bias against the red men was shown by his lack of patience with the idle speculations of Europeans about them, it did not extend to the legendary white inhabitants on the American continent; he devoted considerable space to the Carthaginians, Danes, and the mythical Welsh.[26] As a matter of fact he made a special visit to Louisville for the purpose of collecting information about the Welsh Indians.[27] There he met with a club whose members were interested in gathering facts about the Indians; and after several members of the club—James Harrison, General George Rogers Clark, Dr. Alexander Skinner, Captain James Patten, Major John Harrison, John Sanders, and others—had told of their encounters with the myth, Filson began to speak on the subject. According to tradition his speech was longer than all the others put together, and he went into so great detail about the civil wars in Wales that he never got his Welsh immigrants embarked on the high seas. Finally, he discovered that all the members of his audience except Dr. Skinner were asleep. Mortified, he sat down and was consoled by Dr. Skinner with the remark that his hearers were spellbound by his eloquence.

In his *Kentucke,* Filson repeated the legend of Madoc, son of Owen Gwynnedh, Prince of Wales, who "dissatisfied with the situation of affairs at home, left his country, as related by the Welsh historians, in quest of new settlements, and leaving Ireland to the North, proceeded West till he discovered a fertile country; where, leaving a colony, he returned, and per-

[25] F. S. C. Northrop, *The Meeting of East and West* (New York, Macmillan Company, 1946), 69.

[26] The origins of the mysterious American peoples continued to intrigue writers as late as 1836 at least, when Constantine Rafinesque, another colorful and famous Kentuckian, wrote his *American Nations.* See Richard Ellsworth Call, *The Life and Writings of Rafinesque* (Filson Club *Publications,* no. 10, Louisville, 1895). See also Reuben T. Durrett, *Traditions of the Earliest Visits of Foreigners* (Filson Club *Publications,* no. 23, Louisville, 1908).

[27] Durrett, *Traditions of the Earliest Visits of Foreigners,* 48.

suading many of his country-men to join him, put to sea with ten ships, and was never more heard of."[28] In order to keep the mystery alive, he concluded that this story perhaps had been classified as false all too rashly, for "Western settlers have received frequent accounts of a nation, inhabiting at a great distance up to Missouri, in manners and appearance resembling the other Indians, but speaking Welsh, and retaining some ceremonies of the christian worship." And he named one witness: "Captain Abraham Chaplain, of Kentucke, a gentleman, whose veracity may be entirely depended upon, assured the author, that in the late war, being with his company in garrison at Kaskasky, some Indians came there, and, speaking in the Welsh dialect, were perfectly understood and conversed with by two Welshmen in his company, and that they informed him of the situation of their nation as mentioned above."[29]

Such stories were at that time subject to ridicule, a fact of which Filson was aware; but he prided himself on having called the attention of mankind once more to a topic that had not been settled.[30] Having read Charlevoix, he was aware that the origin of the legend of the Welsh Indians was based on the old Welsh Chronicle in the history of Carodog. Continued reports from the unknown heartland of America about the survivors of this ancient migration would stir the imagination of his readers.

Closing the Appendix with a prophecy, Filson rode ahead at full rein in his prediction of a Utopia. Here in Kentucky,

28 *Kentucke,* 95. 29 *Ibid.,* 96.

30 If Filson had not read David Powell, *The Historie of Cambria, now called Wales,* 1584 (see reprint of 1811, London, James Harding, 166-67), he had read Charlevoix's statement "Il rapporte à ce sujet ce qui est marqué dans l'Histoire du Pays de Galles, écrite par le Docteur DAVID POWEL, sous l'année 1170. Madoc, dit cet Historien, un des Fils du Prince OWEN GUYNETH, las & rebutè des Guerres Civiles, qui s'étoient élevées entre ses Freres après la mort de leur Pere, arma plusieurs Vaisseaux, les pourvut de tout ce qui étoit nécessaire pour un voyage de long cours, & alla chercher de nouvelles Terres à l'Occident de l'Irlande. Il en trouva des très fertiles, & qui n'étoient point habitées: il y débarqua une partie de son Monde, puis retourna en Angleterre, où il fit de nouvelles Recruës, qu'il mena dans sa Colonie." Charlevoix, III, 20.

Nature had finally made reparation for the hardships mankind had endured; here there would be rich harvests for the poor and joyous freedom for the oppressed:

> The recital of your happiness will call to your country all the unfortunate of the earth, who, having experienced oppression, political or religious, will there find a deliverance from their chains. To you innumerable multitudes will emigrate from the hateful regions of despotism and tyranny; and you will surely welcome them as friends, as brothers; you will welcome them to partake with you of your happiness.—Let the memory of Lycurgus, the Spartan legislator, who banished covetousness, and the love of gold from his country; the excellent Locke, who first taught the doctrine of toleration; the venerable Penn, the first who founded a city of brethren; and Washington, the defender and protector of persecuted liberty, be ever the illustrious examples of your political conduct. Avail yourselves of the benefits of nature, and of the fruitful country you inhabit.
>
> In your country, like the land of promise, flowing with milk and honey, a land of brooks of water, of fountains and depths, that spring out of valleys and hills, a land of wheat and barley, and all kinds of fruits, you shall eat bread without scarceness, and not lack any thing in it; where you are neither chilled with the cold of capricorn, nor scorched with the burning heat of cancer; the mildness of your air so great, that you neither feel the effects of infectious fogs, nor pestilential vapours. Thus, your country, favored with the smiles of heaven, will probably be inhabited by the first people the world ever knew.[31]

The immediate reception of the book was encouraging, and Filson planned a second edition. To the inhabitants of the eastern seaboard with its exhausted and crowded farmlands, to the independent but poverty-stricken recent immigrants, to the dispossessed in the Old World as well as the new, this description of Kentucky opened up the prospect of a new life. Dreams and fancies, already lively with the promise of a new and independent nation, were further quickened by Filson's prophecy of a new state, another Eden, where there were un-

[31] *Kentucke,* 108-109.

doubted material riches as well as inviolable personal liberty.

Filson remained in and near Philadelphia after the publication of his book with the hope that he could persuade General Washington to endorse a second edition. Washington, who had extensive lands on the upper reaches of the Ohio, was interested in the establishment of routes of commerce between the Ohio valley and the eastern seaboard. Therefore, on November 30, 1784, Filson wrote Washington a letter in which he told the retired General about the book and map, and expressed a hope that he would be able to visit him at Mount Vernon:

Philadelphia, Novr. 30th. 1784

Sir

Permit me in these lines to express that perfect respect which I with my fellow Citizens of the United States owe to your excellency; I inform you Sir, that I have the pleasure to be the author of a late publication entitled a history and Map of Kentucke; the map I made bold to dedicate to the honourable Congress and your Excelly.; these Sir I request and presume you will patronise. I have sent a number to Colo. Harvey in Richmond and Mr. John Page Esqr. at Rosewell to sell. I have directed Mr. Page to present you with a book and Map you will do me the honour to Receive it I hope one day to Visit you in your retirement from the hurry of life, and find you perfectly enjoying that happiness which your Virtue and the great disposer of all your acts can only reward you with.

I am sir your most obedient humble Sert.

John Filson.[32]

Four days later, on December 4, the impetuous Filson wrote a second and longer letter to Washington and apologized for his being so bold as to suggest a visit with the General, but asked him to write a letter endorsing his work that he might use for a second edition:

[32] Letters in the Manuscript Division, Library of Congress; published in full in P. Lee Phillips, *The First Map of Kentucky by John Filson* (Washington, W. H. Lowdermilk & Company, 1908), 11-16.

This impression of 1500 [copies] have in the Course of a few weeks met with a rapid sale, which encourages me to offer the publick a second edition of this book, which I intend in the Course of this Winter. I lately had the pleasure to be acquainted with Mr. Claybourn a gentleman from Richmond, with whom I suppose you are acquainted; I informed him of my intentions, at which Mr. Claybourn expressed his sattisfaction, desiring me to write requesting you Sir, to form your sentiments in a letter indicative of the probability and Convenience of a Communication in trade, with the eastern & western waters, by the sources of [the] Potomac, and the waters that form the Aleghany, particularly Cheat river; a publication of this nature he said would Certainly be sattisfactory to you, I therefore request you sir, if agreeable, to be explicit on the subject and send it to me at Dunlaps printing office in this City, with all convenient expedition, which you may depend I shall add in your own Sentiments to this my second edition of the Kentucke history, which I intend Commiting to the press about Christmas, perhaps I may delay a few days for your letter if it Come not before that time.[33]

Washington replied on January 16, 1785. He expressed a keen interest in a map of the western territory but admonished Filson that the map should be based on actual surveys. Since he had not yet received the book and map which the author had sent him, he could not express his opinion of the work.[34]

Upon receipt of this letter, Filson hastened to write General Washington a third time. In a letter dated February 8 he told Washington that he was enclosing a copy of the book and the map, and that he would wait until March for an expression of opinion that he might use in his second edition.[35] The second and last letter from Washington was brief and courteous. He acknowledged the receipt of the book and the map, but said nothing directly about an endorsement: "Taking it for granted you must have received it [his letter of January 16] 'ere this, I beg leave to refer to its contents, as aught I could say on the subject would be only repetition."[36]

Washington's refusal to endorse the work apparently dashed

[33] *Ibid.,* 11-13. [34] *Ibid.,* 14-15. [35] *Ibid.,* 13-14. [36] *Ibid.,* 15-16.

Filson's hopes of the success of a second edition. While no second edition appeared in America, the year following saw the book published in both France and Germany. The most famous of these was the French edition, entitled *Histoire de Kentucke, Nouvelle Colonie A L'Ouest de la Virginie,* translated by Mr. Parraud and published by Buisson.[37] The French edition differed from the American in the following respects: the endorsement of Boone, Todd, and Harrod was placed at the very end of the book, and a preface by the translator was substituted in its original position; and the tables of distances at the end were omitted and several new pieces added.[38]

The first German edition, entitled *Reise Nach Kentucke und Nachrichten von dieser neu angebaueten landschaft in Nordamerika* was translated by Heinrich Bronner and published in Frankfurt in 1785.[39] Two printings or editions followed: one in Nürnberg in 1789;[40] and a second in 1790 in Leipzig.[41]

In England and the United States this first work on Kentucky and Daniel Boone had a long history. For more than a century it was purloined and plagiarized. In 1786 one Alexander

37 *Histoire de Kentucke, Nouvelle Colonie A L'Ouest de La Virginie;* Contenant, 1. La Découverte, l'Acquisition, l'Établissement, la Description topographique, l'Histoire naturelle, & c. du Territoire: 2. la Relation historique du Colonel Boon, un des premiers Colons, sur les guerres contre les Naturels: 3. l'Assemblée des Piankashaws au Poste Saint Vincent; 4. un exposé succinct des Nations Indiennes qui habitent dans les limites des Treize États-Unis, de leurs Moeurs & Coutumes, & des Réflexions sur leur origine; & autres Pièces: Avec Une Carte. Ouvrage pour servir de suite aux LETTRES D'UN CULTIVATEUR AMÉRICAIN. Traduit de l'Anglois, de M. John Filson; Par M. Parraud, De l'Académie des Arcades de Rome. A Paris, Chez Buisson, Libraire, Hotel de Mesgrigny, rue des Poitevins, no. 13, 1785. Avec Approbation et Permission.

38 Pp. 146-231. Déclaration Du Congrès, Concernant l'érection des nouveaux Etats dans les terres de l'Ouest; Ordonnance Du Congrès Pour déterminer la manière dont il fera disposé des terres de l'ouest des Etats-Unis; Passages De Diodore de Sicile, d'Aristote, de Platon, d'Elien & de Plutarque, qui prouvent que l'Amérique étoit connue des Anciens; Du Gouvernement des Sauvages, De leurs Conseils, de leur Eloquence Discours choisis; Extrait De La Relation Du Capitaine Isaac Stewart.

39 Jillson, *Filson's Kentucke,* 154.

40 Published by Schneider und Weigel. See Wilhelm Heinsius, *Allegemeines Bücher-Lexikon* (19 vols., Leipzig, 1812-1894), I, 881.

41 Published by C. Weigel und Schneider. Copy in the Library of Congress.

Fitzroy prepared and published *The Discovery, Purchase, and Settlement of the Country of Kentuckie in North America,* which was a plagiarized account of Filson's work without the Boone narrative.[42] The next year an altered and abridged version of the "Adventures of Colonel Daniel Boon" appeared in *The American Museum, or Repository of Ancient and Modern Fugitive Pieces;*[43] and Gilbert Imlay's work, entitled *A Topographical Description of the Western Territory of North America* and published in London, New York, and Dublin in the 1790's, included Filson's work.[44] A London edition of Filson's work appeared in 1793 with a map drawn by Thomas Hutchins.[45] As late as 1902 Daniel Boone's biographers were still publishing Filson's story of the Kentucky pioneer.[46]

This little volume, which sold originally for one dollar and a half, is now one of the rarest items of Americana. Only a few well-preserved copies of the Wilmington edition exist: Yale University owns a copy in its original binding; there is a copy with the deckle edges complete in the American Philosophical Society in Philadelphia; George Washington's copy, which Filson hoped would bring an endorsement for a second edition, is in the Boston Athenaeum; and the copy Filson gave his friend Boone is now in the Free Library in Philadelphia.[47] If Washington had endorsed a second edition, it is likely that the value of the first would be much less than it is today.

42 Printed by H. Goldney, 15 Pater Noster Row, London.

43 (Philadelphia, 1787), II, 321-28.

44 London, 1792, 1793, 1797; Dublin, 1793; New York, 1793.

45 Printed for J. Stockdale.

46 Cecil B. Hartley, *The Life and Times of Colonel Daniel Boone* (New York, Perkins Book Company, 1902), 357-85.

47 R. C. Ballard Thruston, "Filson's History and Map of Kentucky," *Filson Club History Quarterly,* VIII (1934), 1-38.

Chapter 5 Boone's Story

AMERICANS and Europeans alike read the story of Daniel Boone's adventures in Kentucky almost as soon as the Indian wars were over. In his book on Kentucky, Filson allowed Boone thirty-three pages[1] in which to recite the epic of the transformation of the wilderness into a peaceful habitation for man. By publishing the narrative he not only insured the immortality of Boone,[2] but at the same time he created the prototype of the American hero.[3]

The "Adventures of Col. Daniel Boon" was the most popular chapter in Filson's book, and in it he did his best writing. Probably because of these facts, a "shabby report"[4] has come down to us that Filson did not write the Boone narrative, one of those contemporary rumors that found its way into the written records where it has been successively discovered to plague historians. Since the fame of Filson has always rested on rather slender foundations, to deny him the authorship of the Boone narrative would detract seriously from his reputation. Among the three or four accomplishments that have saved him from oblivion, the Boone story ranks high. Furthermore, because it is an important chronicle in the history of the United States, a careful investigation should be made of every shred of evidence bearing on its authorship.

When Colonel Durrett was writing his biography of Filson

in 1884, he wrote to Lyman Draper, that pottering but diligent collector of frontier records[5] who was then associated with the State Historical Society of Wisconsin. Draper, who at that time had spent more than fifty years collecting the records of the neglected heroes of the frontier, replied that he had failed to learn much about Filson, although he had tried to do so;[6] but he did report the doubt that had been cast on Filson's having written the famous Boone memoir.

Yet among the manuscript notes of the late Rev. John D. Shane, which I have—I find this statement, which he derived from Josiah Collins of Bath Co., Ky.—Collins came to Ky. in 1778.

Boone's Filson was written by Humphrey Marshall. Boone lived at that time at the Cross Plains (Boone's Station—Now Athens, Fayette Co. L. C. D.), 10 miles from Lexington. Gen. Calmees and I had a conversation about some statements in that (work), & he said Humphrey Marshall was to blame about that & that he ought not to have written it. It was always understood that H. M. (Marshall) wrote Boone's statement as published by Filson. This is all Collins is recorded to have said on the subject.

I would judge if Filson did write the Boone narrative, that he got Marshall to brush it up; for it is garnished with what seems to me, some of Marshall's floridity, & not found in the rest of Filson's work. At this period, 1783-84, Boone was a Deputy Surveyor under Col. Tom Marshall—& no doubt Boone into frequent [contact] with the Colonel's Son, Humphrey Marshall.[7]

1 *Kentucke,* 49-82.

2 John Gilmer Speed, "Kentucky's Centennial," *Harpers Weekly,* XXXVI (1892), 546.

3 Jay B. Hubbell, *The South in American Literature, 1607-1900* (Durham, N. C., Duke University Press, 1950), 315.

4 Durrett, *John Filson,* 43.

5 William B. Hesseltine, *Pioneer's Mission: The Story of Lyman Copeland Draper* (Madison, State Historical Society of Wisconsin, 1954).

6 That the interest in Filson was beginning to revive some ten years before Colonel Durrett's biography was published is indicated by an article, signed S. G. D., in the *American Historical Record* for October, 1874. It began, "The question has frequently been asked: who was John Filson?" Draper Mss. 10CC1-34; microfilm copy in the Princeton University Library.

7 Letter dated March 23, 1884, reproduced in full in Thruston, "Filson's History and Map of Kentucky," 4. Draper Mss. 12CC73; microfilm copy in the

Colonel Durrett, like all other historians who have investigated the report, refused to accept the statement of Josiah Collins, although he considered it quite possible that the manuscript might have been submitted to Marshall for correction in grammar and punctuation.[8]

In interpreting Collins' statement, Colonel Durrett (and possibly Draper) has overlooked the fact that when Collins referred to "Boone's Filson"—an unaccountable juxtaposition of words—and to "Boone's statement as published by Filson," he was in all probability referring to the entire book on Kentucky and not to the Boone narrative alone. In the letter to Colonel Durrett, Draper wrote that the Boone narrative "is garnished with what seems to me, some of Marshall's floridity, & not found in the rest of Filson's work." By "the rest of Filson's work" he obviously meant the manuscripts Filson left as a result of his two journeys to Vincennes,[9] or Post St. Vincent as it was then called, and not to the other sections of his *Kentucke*. Only by this sort of comparison can the Boone narrative be said to have greater "floridity," and even then the difference is not striking. Certainly the most florid writing in Filson's book on Kentucky occurs in some of the descriptive passages and in his prophecy.[10] Furthermore, in at least one reference to Filson's work, made in 1824, apparently the whole book on Kentucky is referred to as the "Boone Narrative";[11] and in view of the popularity of this chapter it is not at all improbable that such practice was fairly common. Thus the doubt cast by the report threatens to become completely devas-

---

Princeton University Library. This interview is included among several others with Josiah Collins, who had come to Boonesborough, Kentucky, in 1778.

8 Durrett, *John Filson*, 44.

9 "Two Westward Journeys," ed. by Beverley W. Bond, Jr., *Mississippi Valley Historical Review*, IX (1922-1923), 320-30; "Defeat on the Wabash," ed. by Leonard Clinton Helderman, *Filson Club History Quarterly*, XII (1938), 187-99; and two manuscripts in the Draper Collection, which are mainly rough notes on which "Two Westward Journeys" is based.

10 *Kentucke*, 107-109.

11 See Humphrey Marshall's statement below.

tating to Filson's reputation as an author, for it probably should be interpreted "Did Humphrey Marshall write Filson's *Kentucke?*" Fortunately for Filson, there is no evidence other than this one statement for such a possibility, and there is a great deal against it.

Humphrey Marshall, an irascible Tory and a controversial figure in early Kentucky politics, wrote a history of Kentucky in 1812[12] in which he defended some of his political views.[13] He republished his history in 1824, and in the preface to this second edition he refers explicitly to Filson as the author of the Boone narrative: "In the composition of the work, the materials have been drawn, from conversation with the first settlers—my own observations and experiences—Burck's History of Virginia—Boone's Narrative of 1784, by Filson; and public documents of various descriptions, to which I have had access."[14] Moreover, Marshall never indicated in any of his writings that he had aided Filson in his work.

If the evidence given needs any corroboration, one can find it in the candor and guilelessness of John Filson. Of those who helped him with his book and map, he is lavish in his acknowledgments. It seems extremely unlikely that he would fail to give credit to Humphrey Marshall if any were due. It is true, however, that the Boone narrative does show some improvement in style over the rest of Filson's book, but the difference is not great enough to suspect different authorship. The intrinsic nature of the narrative form lends itself to more coherent organization than the miscellaneous material that is included in the other sections, but the superiority in style has been exaggerated.[15] In comparison with Filson's other work,

12 *The History of Kentucky* (Frankfort, Henry Gore, 1812). Next to Filson's *Kentucke,* this is the rarest and most sought history of the state.

13 Clark, *A History of Kentucky,* 383. See also, *Dictionary of American Biography,* XII, 309-10.

14 *The History of Kentucky* (2 vols., Frankfort, George S. Robinson, 1824), I, v.

15 Durrett, *John Filson,* 43; Jillson, *Filson's Kentucke,* 153.

however, the *Kentucke* is much better in both grammar and style, but this difference may be accounted for by the fact that it was prepared for publication. Also, James Adams, the printer, had a reputation for the "regularity, neatness, and correctness of his printing."[16]

As to the question of how the name of Humphrey Marshall became associated with Filson's work, two conjectures which appear plausible are submitted. First, Marshall was thoroughly disliked by many of his contemporaries for his Tory views,[17] and they may have attributed many things to him which they did not like. Thus, he could have been a convenient scapegoat for any objectionable statements—Shane in his interview with Collins does not indicate what they were—in Filson's book.

The second conjecture has been made before.[18] In Bradford Township, Chester County, there lived in 1784 Humphry Marshall, a celebrated American naturalist[19] who was working on a book of his own. This book, a manual on American trees and shrubs, was published in 1785 under the title *Arbustum Americanum*.[20] His home, "Marshallton," was on the Strasburg Road not more than ten or twelve miles from Filson's Chester County home, and on the direct route from East Fallowfield to Philadelphia. Filson must have known this "quiet Quaker of West Bradford's hills," and it is possible that he took his manuscript to him before he went on to his publisher in Wilmington. Marshall would have been interested in any information about the flora of Kentucky, and if he did see the manuscript, he might have given the author the benefit of some literary criticism. It is also possible that Filson upon his return

16 Obituary of James Adams in the Philadelphia *Pennsylvania Gazette*, December 29, 1792.

17 Collins, *History of Kentucky*, I, 282.

18 Wilson, "John Filson in Pennsylvania," 197-98.

19 See William Darlington, *Memorials of John Bartram and Humphry Marshall* (Philadelphia, Lindsay & Blakiston, 1849), 485-93.

20 Actually the title was misspelled *Arbustrum Americanum: The American Grove* (Philadelphia, J. Crukshank, 1785).

to Kentucky mentioned that Humphry Marshall had assisted him with the manuscript, thereby giving currency to the rumor that Humphrey Marshall of Kentucky had something to do with writing the book.

Since the evidence is conclusive that Filson wrote the Boone narrative as well as the rest of the first book about Kentucky, to him must be given the credit for realizing the literary possibilities in the story of Boone's adventures. Doubtless Boone would have had his biographers anyway, but in Filson he had the equivalent of a modern press agent. And on this first report the Boone legend has been built. The extent to which this legend has entered into American life can hardly be overstated. More than any other hero, Boone has become a part of our national folklore, and subsequent heroes, such as Davy Crockett, Kit Carson, and Paul Bunyan have been cast in the same mold. In addition to the biographies and stories devoted exclusively to Boone's life—and there are some fifty listed in a recent bibliography[21]—he has been the inspiration for a substantial portion of American literature. As early as 1813 he had achieved a legendary status and was cavorting with supernatural powers. In a grandiose epic published that year we find that Boone had been selected by a heavenly messenger for the settlement of the West:

> With meteor-swiftness, from the council dome,
> High through the azure heights of Atmosphere,
> His lofty way the mission'd Seraph winged;
> Till poised above the Carolinian hills,
> He sought with searching view, th' adventurous Boone[22]

Not only in regional and contemporary pieces but also in the great and enduring literature of this country Boone has

21 J. Winston Coleman, Jr., *A Bibliography of Kentucky History* (Lexington, University of Kentucky Press, 1949), 103-109.

22 Daniel Bryan, *The Mountain Muse: Comprising the Adventures of Daniel Boone and the Power of Virtue and Refined Beauty* (Harrisonburg, Va., Davidson & Bourne, 1813), Book II, p. 51.

had a significant place. As the prototype of the American hero, who incidentally embodied many of the virtues of the European natural man, Boone has directly and indirectly been responsible for many of the characters in American fiction. One of the first writers who became indebted to this legend was James Fenimore Cooper, whose Leatherstocking bore unmistakable similarities to Boone. In *The Pioneers,* the first novel (1823) in which Leatherstocking appeared, the hero preferred the simple hunting life of the forests to the complicated and artificial mores of civilized society. In subsequent novels, particularly in *The Last of the Mohicans,* events in the life of Boone furnished Cooper with some of the details for his stories.[23] Many other American writers, ranging all the way from Walt Whitman to A. B. Guthrie, Jr., have exploited the Boone legend. As the architect of this legend, Filson made an incalculable contribution to the folklore, the ideals, and the literature of America.[24]

Whatever influence the Boone legend had abroad must be attributed to Filson. Since his book was published in France, Germany, and England, Europeans knew of Boone's exploits only a year later than Americans. Especially the French, with their interest in things exotic, must have found in this work a concrete and grand example of the natural hero.

In orotund prose that certainly bore the stamp of Filson

23 "Although Boone was not exactly the prototype of Cooper's Leatherstocking, there is a haunting similarity between the two figures. Cooper based a part of Chapters X and XII of *The Last of the Mohicans* on a well known exploit of Boone in conducting the rescue of Betsey and Fannie Calloway and Jemima Boone, his daughter, from the Cherokees." Henry Nash Smith, *Virgin Land,* (Cambridge, Mass., Harvard University Press, 1950), 59. This work contains an excellent account of the Boone legend in American letters. See particularly Chapters V and VI.

24 Although plagiarized accounts of Boone's story were published, it was not until 1833 that a full length biography of Boone appeared. See Timothy Flint, *Biographical Memoir of Daniel Boone: the First Settler of Kentucky* (Cincinnati, Guilford and Company). That Boone deserved the fame he has enjoyed has been seriously questioned. See Clarence Walworth Alvord, "The Daniel Boone Myth," *Journal of the Illinois State Historical Society,* XIX (1926), 16-30.

rather than Boone,[25] the hero of the Indian wars began his narrative by stating that he and his family were living on the Yadkin River in North Carolina when a curiosity that "is natural to the soul of man" led him into the wilderness of Kentucky. This natural curiosity must have been uncommonly strong in the Boone family. Daniel's grandfather, George Boone, was an English Quaker who migrated from his native Devon to Bucks County, Pennsylvania.[26] Daniel's father, Squire Boone, started the trek westward by moving to Oley Township (later in Berks County) where Daniel was born in 1734. Fifteen years later the family moved southward into the Shenandoah, where they spent a year or so living near an old friend and neighbor, John Lincoln, whose great-grandson Abraham was to become the most famous of the Kentuckians. From the Shenandoah the Boones moved on to the less-promising Valley of the Yadkin, whence Daniel was to set out for Kentucky.

At the time Filson wrote the biography Boone was fifty years old, a plausible age for reflecting on his role in the course of empire: "The settling of this region well deserves a place in history. Most of the memorable events I have myself been exercised in; and, for the satisfaction of the public, will briefly relate the circumstances of my adventures, and scenes of life, from my first movement to this country until this day."[27] It is barely possible that Filson was engaging in some dry humor when he has this roving woodsman begin his story with: "It was on the first of May, in the year 1769, that I resigned my domestic happiness for a time, and left my family and peaceful habitation on the Yadkin River, in North-Carolina, to wander

[25] Boone apparently acquiesced in the pretense that Filson had merely written down what he, Boone, had said. Years later, while living in Missouri and when the Indian wars were only a memory, he is reported to have asked that the story be read aloud to him repeatedly and to have commented: "All true! Every word true! Not a lie in it." John Bakeless, *Daniel Boone* (New York, William Morrow & Company, 1939), 395.

[26] *Ibid.*, 3-14.

[27] *Kentucke*, 50.

through the wilderness of America, in quest of the country of Kentucke . . ."[28] since there is certainly no evidence to indicate that Boone ever suffered any nostalgia for peaceful domesticity. But since Filson was devoid of a sense of humor, it must have been an incredible naiveté or the customary punctilious regard for the conventions that led him to begin the story with Boone's expression of regret. Perhaps Daniel had remembered that his wife Rebecca had objected to his wandering off on a trip that was both unnecessary and uncertain at the season of the year when farm work was urgent and heavy. Perhaps she had resorted to, "What will people say?" Out of fairness to her, when he spoke for the record, he made it clear that his reason for leaving home was Homeric rather than domestic.

Boone and his companions, John Finlay, John Stewart, Joseph Holden, James Monay, and William Cool, wandered about Kentucky in peace until December 22, 1769 (?). On that day he and John Stewart, while on "a pleasing ramble," were captured by some Indians who rushed out of a canebrake upon them. For seven days they were held prisoners. At the end of that time Boone gently woke his companion, and both stole away to their camp in the dead of the night "when sleep had locked the senses" of their captors. There they found their companions "dispersed and gone home" but in their stead, Daniel's brother Squire, who with another adventurer had come from North Carolina in search of Daniel. He had arrived at an auspicious time, for the Indians, who resented the escape of their prisoners, recaptured John Stewart within a few days and killed him. In the same sentence in which he told of Stewart's death, Boone said "and the man that came with my brother returned home by-himself."[29]

[28] *Ibid.,* 50-51.

[29] *Ibid.,* 53. The man, Alexander Neely, was apparently killed by the Indians, for his skeleton was supposed to have been found long afterward in a hollow tree. Cotterill, *History of Pioneer Kentucky,* 53.

Daniel was pleased to see his brother and to share with him some of the natural and simple joys of the life in the wilderness: "Thus situated, many hundred miles from our families in the howling wilderness, I believe few would have equally enjoyed the happiness we experienced. I often observed to my brother, You see now how little nature requires to be satisfied. Felicity, the companion of content, is rather found in our own breasts than in the enjoyment of external things: And I firmly believe it requires but a little philosophy to make a man happy in whatsoever state he is."[30]

Here is the natural man, innately good, freed from the tensions of society and from the shackles of convention, finding supreme happiness in the simple life. That these were Boone's own words few believed; but that they expressed his philosophy was assumed by the readers who elected Boone the popular hero of the Romantic Revolution. Chinard, a student of the American influence on French literature, has marveled at Boone's philosophical powers and has distinguished him from the French *"philosophes en chambre."* Since Chinard apparently did not know that Filson wrote the story of Boone's adventures, his bewilderment at the old Indian fighter's penchant for philosophizing is understandable.[31]

30 *Kentucke,* 53-54.

31 "Si Boone est un philosophe, il ne faut pas le confondre avec nos philosophes en chambre; l'homme reste singulièrment rude et même barbare à certains moments. Un peu plus loin, on voit qu'il n'hésiste pas imiter les Indiens, à scalper ses ennemis et à rapporter leurs chevelures comme de glorieux trophées." Gilbert Chinard, *L'Exotisme Américain dans l'Oeuvre de Chateaubrand* (Paris, Libraire Hachette et Cie., 1918), 98.

Chinard quotes a passage from the Boone narrative (pp. 54-56 in Filson's *Kentucke*) which he took from Imlay, 1792, London edition. He does not mention Filson and obviously thought the words were Boone's: "Un jour, dit le vieux colonel Boone, le pionnier du Kentucky dont nous avons déjà parlé, j'enterpris un voyage dans le pays" (p. 97). At the end of the quotation, Chinard writes somewhat condescendingly: "Il serait fort injuste de comparer les mérites littéraires de Boone et de Chateaubriand. Le vieux solitaire n'est pourtant pas si gauche qu'on pourrait le croire; ces vieux pionniers américains que ne connaissaient qu'un seul livre, la Bible, ont souvent une fermeté de style qui étonne. Mais l'utilité première de tels rapprochements est de nous servir

Thirty years later the speech quoted above was paraphrased in a minor epic about the same hero:

> My Brother! Now we see what a rich fount
> Of pure felicity the mind of man
> Within itself contains, if not defiled
> By the corruptions of soul-blackening Vice.
> How little on the gew-gaw glare of Wealth,
> On Power's pageant pomp, and vain parade,
> The human heart for happiness depends.[32]

Although Filson surely was writing with an eye on the romantic mood of his readers, he should not be criticized too severely for distorting the character of his subject. In two other contemporary accounts Boone lived up to the romantic ideal. In 1770 a party of forty hunters came through the Cumberland Gap into Kentucky, some nine of whom proceeded as far west as the Green River. One day while encamped and believing that they were alone in the country, they were startled by the sound of a human voice raised in song not far from their camp. Approaching cautiously in the direction of the sound they soon saw a white man stretched full length on the ground, singing as loudly as he could. It was Daniel Boone, who was probably surprised that he was not the only white man in Kentucky.[33] The second account described Boone as a man with "a remarkably pleasant temper, nothing appeared to ruffle his mind, or make him uneasy, of a pleasant countenance."[34]

Squire Boone returned to North Carolina on the first of May, 1770, leaving Daniel alone in Kentucky. Never, confessed Daniel, had he been under any greater necessity of exercising philosophy and fortitude: "The idea of a beloved wife and family, and their anxiety upon the account of my absence and

---

à démontier l'authenticité des sentiments de Chateaubriand, ce qui est av moins aussi nécessaire que de retrouver l'itinéraire qu'il a suivi" (p. 98).

32 Bryan, 128.

33 Draper Mss., "Life of Daniel Boone," III, 64; quoted in Cotterill, 55.

34 Draper Mss. 12CC73; microfilm copy in the Princeton University Library.

exposed situation, made sensible impressions on my heart."[35] However, he failed to explain why it was necessary for him to remain in Kentucky; instead, he hastened to report how the beauties of nature soon "expelled every gloom and vexatious thought." After gaining the summit of a commanding ridge—there is considerable doubt that a spot exists in Kentucky from which all the scenery described below is visible—

and, looking round with astonishing delight, [I] beheld the ample plains, the beauteous tracts below. On the other hand, I surveyed the famous river Ohio that rolled in silent dignity, marking the western boundary of Kentucke with inconceivable grandeur. At a vast distance I beheld the mountains lift their venerable brows, and penetrate the clouds. All things were still. I kindled a fire near a fountain of sweet water, and feasted on the loin of a buck, which a few hours before I had killed. The sullen shades of night soon overspread the whole hemisphere, and the earth seemed to gasp after the hovering moisture. My roving excursion this day had fatigued my body, and diverted my imagination. I laid me down to sleep, and I awoke not until the sun had chased away the night.[36]

It was not until March 25 of the next year that Boone returned to his family in North Carolina. He sold his farm and on September 25, 1773, set out again for Kentucky, accompanied by his own and five other families. A party of forty wilderness scouts joined them on the way as they left their thin farms along the Yadkin to march into the promised land of Kentucky. The enthusiasm of this hopeful beginning, however, soon subsided, for on October 10 they were attacked by Indians. Six men, including Boone's eldest son, fell. This misfortune overtook them as they were approaching the Cumberland Mountains, which Boone described as follows: "The aspect of these cliffs is so wild and horrid, that it is impossible to behold them without terror. The spectator is apt to imagine that nature had formerly suffered some violent convulsion; and

[35] *Kentucke,* 54. [36] *Ibid.,* 55.

that these are the dismembered remains of the dreadful shock; the ruins, not of Persepolis or Palmyra, but of the world!"[37] How this coonskin hero, entirely innocent of letters, knew that Persepolis and Palmyra were in ruins is a minor mystery;[38] but like the romantic natural man of his age he had acquired in contemporary and later accounts an incredible store of classical allusions. If Filson's book was more popular in Versailles than in Boonesborough, it is small wonder.

After this attack by the Indians, Boone stopped with his family on the Clinch River, where he remained until June, 1774. Here Lord Dunmore, the last royal governor of Virginia, asked him to run an 800-mile errand: to proceed to the Falls of the Ohio and conduct a party of surveyors into the interior of Kentucky. Returning to his family after sixty-two days, Boone was immediately placed in charge of three garrisons of Dunmore's troops that were marching against the Shawnee. As soon as this tour of duty was finished, he again undertook the settlement of Kentucky, this time associating himself with Richard Henderson and the famous Transylvania Company.[39] As a result of this association Boone became the founder of the fort that bears his name to this day, now a lonely, somnolent village between the Kentucky River hills, where the events of history are something less than a memory. To the site of Boonesborough he brought his wife Rebecca and his daughter Jemima on June 14, 1775. They were "the first white women that ever stood on the banks of Kentucke river."[40]

The Indians persisted in their attempts to harass the settlers out of the land; and on July 14, 1776, they captured Boone's daughter and the two daughters of Colonel Calloway. Boone and eight men from the fort immediately pursued them and

[37] *Ibid.*, 58.

[38] Durrett says "it may be doubted if he could distinguish these ancient cities from Gog and Magog." *John Filson*, 37.

[39] See Cotterill, 71-94.

[40] *Kentucke*, 60.

two days later overtook the party, killed two of the Indians, and rescued the girls.[41]

With the coming of reinforcements from North Carolina and a band of a hundred Virginians whom the Indians feared (calling them the Long Knives) open warfare ceased; but the red men continued their insidious forms of annoyance. On February 7, 1778, while he was engaged in making salt at the Blue Licks, Boone and twenty-seven other pioneers were captured by the Indians. He was taken to old Chillicothe on the Little Miami River and from there to Detroit, where the British Governor Henry Hamilton offered a hundred pounds sterling for his release.[42] The Indians refused the offer and took Boone back to their camp on the Little Miami, where as a captive he lived a life far different from that of prisoners in modern wars:

At Chelicothe I spent my time as comfortably as I could expect; was adopted, accordin to their custom, into a family where I became a son, and had a great share in the affection of my new parents, brothers, sisters, and friends. I was exceedingly familiar and friendly with them, always appearing as chearful and satisfied as possible, and they put great confidence in me. I often went hunting

[41] This famous frontier incident had an unusually romantic side, as three of the men in Boone's party—Holden, Henderson, and Calloway—were fiancés of the girls. Cotterill, 105.

[42] What transactions Boone entered into with the British while he was in Detroit has been a matter of much discussion. After the siege of Boonesborough, Colonel Calloway charged that Boone had been guilty of treason at Detroit and had encouraged the British to support the Indians in their invasion of Kentucky. Although Boone was acquitted, his behavior was somewhat suspicious both at Detroit and with the besiegers of Boonesborough. Governor Hamilton, in a letter to General Carleton, dated April 25, 1778, wrote: "By Boone's account the people on the frontiers have been incessantly harrassed by parties of Indians they have not been able to sow grain at all Kentucke will not have a morsel of bread by the middle of June. Cloathing is not to be had, nor do they expect relief from Congress—their dilemma will probably induce them to trust to the savages who have shewn such humanity to their prisoners, & come to this place before winter." *Report of the Pioneer and Historical Society of the State of Michigan,* IX (1886), 935. For an interesting account of Boone's alleged treason see Bakeless, Chapter XII, "Treasons or Stratagems."

with them, and frequently gained their applause for my activity at our shooting-matches. I was careful not to exceed many of them in shooting; for no people are more envious than they in this sport. —The Shawanese king took great notice of me, and treated me with profound respect, and entire friendship, often entrusting me to hunt at my liberty.[43]

Returning from a hunting trip one day, Boone was alarmed to find that 450 choice Shawnee warriors were planning to march against Boonesborough. He escaped just before sunrise one morning and made his way to the fort, a journey of 160 miles during which he had only one meal. On August 8 the Indian band appeared before the gates. The 450 braves were there, commanded by a mythical Captain Duquesne and eleven other French officers from Canada.[44] With British and French colors flying, they marched back and forth, and finally sent a summons to Boone to surrender in the name of his Britannic majesty. Boone asked for a period of two days to consider the matter, during which time feverish preparations for defense were made within the garrison; and at the end of the period, Boone returned the answer "that we were determined to defend our fort while a man was living—Now, said I to their commander, who stood attentively hearing my sentiments, We laugh at all your formidable preparations: But thank you for giving us notice and time to provide for our defence. Your efforts will not prevail; for our gates shall for ever deny you admittance."[45]

The hero had defied the enemy. After attempts at subter-

[43] *Kentucke,* 64-65.

[44] Bakeless, 202, says that De Quindre was the Canadian commander and that he was accompanied by an interpreter by the name Chêne. Boone was probably confused by the two French names and Filson wrote down Duquesne. A list of officers in the Indian Department, District of Detroit, for September 5, 1788, includes the names of Isidore Chesne and Antoine and Francois Dequindre, but no Duquesne. *Report of the Pioneer and Historical Society of the State of Michigan,* IX (1886), 470.

[45] *Kentucke,* 68. For another account of Boone's action in this instance, see Cotterill, 141-46.

fuge and a nine-day assault failed to take the fort, the enemy raised the siege and departed.

The crescendo of the Indian wars increased as station after station was attacked. On August 15, 1782, about five hundred Indians and Canadian French attacked Bryan's Station, near Lexington. In language strangely reminiscent of Caesar's Gallic Wars, Boone describes the battle: "Without demanding a surrender, they furiously assaulted the garrison, which was happily prepared to oppose them; and, after they had expended much ammunition in vain, and killed the cattle round the fort, not being likely to make themselves masters of this place, they raised the seige, and departed in the morning of the third day after they came, with the loss of about thirty killed, and the number of wounded uncertain."[46]

The pursuit of the fleeing savages ended in the bloody Battle of Blue Licks, "the last battle of the Revolution." On one of the rolling hills south of the Licking River overlooking the Blue Licks, the carnage of the fifteen minutes of fierce fighting was ghastly. Sixty white men fell, including two colonels—Todd and Trigg—and Boone's second son. Four of the seven men taken prisoners were barbarously murdered by young warriors being trained in the arts of cruelty. Boone in reflecting on the horror of the battle described the panic and the slaughter, and concluded with the laconic statement, "many widows were now made."

This terrible battle was the end of serious Indian troubles in Kentucky. General Clark's expedition against them beyond the Ohio left them with little taste for further warfare in Kentucky; and "the great king beyond the waters," being disappointed in his expectations, had no more reason to encourage their depredations. The settlement of Kentucky was secure. Boone, reviewing the long and harrowing struggle, reflected on his mission and his sacrifice: "My footsteps have often been

[46] *Kentucke,* 75.

marked with blood. . . . Two darling sons, and a brother, have I lost by savage hands, which have also taken from me forty valuable horses, and abundance of cattle. Many dark and sleepless nights have I been a companion for owls, separated from the chearful society of men, scorched by the Summer's sun, and pinched by the Winter's cold, an instrument ordained to settle the wilderness. But now the scene is changed: Peace crowns the sylvan shade."[47]

One would hardly have been surprised had this wilderness scout closed with a paraphrase of

Tantae molis erat Romanam condere gentem.

[47] *Ibid.,* 80-81.

Chapter 6 The Map

WHILE JAMES Adams was printing John Filson's *Kentucke* in Wilmington, two craftsmen in Philadelphia were at work on his map. They were Henry Pursell, an engraver of Carter's Alley, and Ternon Rook, a printer of South Second Street. Patience was surely one of their virtues, for Filson made more than thirty corrections in the map during the course of its publication.[1]

The map, which was sold with the book and also separately, made a substantial contribution to the Easterner's knowledge of the land that lay beyond the mountains. During the late eighteenth century this vast domain was viewed largely through the rhetorical haze that had been created by the literary prophets of the West. Lewis Evans, Jonathan Carver, Hector St. John de Crèvecœur, Gilbert Imlay, and the Reverend James Smith were among those who had beheld the vision of a new agrarian society in the West, which would be dominated by the ideals of simplicity, virtue, and contentment.[2] But their descriptions of this Utopia, although dazzling and grandiloquent, were often lacking in geographical detail. No doubt the eminently practical and realistic General Washington had in mind some of these rhetorical flights when he wrote Filson that he would like to see a map of the western territory, but only one based on actual surveys and careful observations.

Since Filson's map was not drawn entirely from actual surveys, it did not meet Washington's rigorous specifications; however, it did much to illumine the haze that had enveloped the mysterious land of Kentucke.[3]

The difficulties involved in drawing a map of Kentucky in 1784 must have appeared well-nigh insurmountable even to a competent surveyor like Filson. Map making under the most favorable conditions is an exacting business, and on the frontier conditions were far from ideal. Kentucky was almost as unknown to Filson as Virginia had been to Captain John Smith in 1608, and there were many of the same perils and hardships for the cartographer. Since Filson had not been commissioned to draw the map, one may well wonder why he did it. No government, geographical society, or land company had employed him or even given him any encouragement to produce a map of Kentucky. The motives that prompted and sustained this bold enterprise were personal, and from the enormity of the task one can well believe that they were unusually powerful.

Cartography, in common with most human enterprises, may be pursued for a variety of reasons. It has flourished, however, when and where the energies of men were directed toward a combination of two interests: the pursuit of commerce and the exploration of the unknown. In America the commercial motive included not only the discovery and improvement of routes of trade but also the promotion of virgin lands. It was for the latter reason that Filson drew his map, despite his rather

1 Thruston, "Filson's History and Map of Kentucky," 23.

2 For an excellent description of this writing, see Smith, *Virgin Land,* 123-32.

3 There had been numerous maps showing a part of the Kentucky country, the earliest of which was made in 1673 by Jacques Marquette; but the only ones that approached being a map devoted exclusively to the Kentucky country were one anonymously drawn in 1776 and entitled *A General Map of the New Settlement Called Transilvania* and Robert Johnson's *A Surveyor's Sketch Map of Kentucky in 1782.* Neither of these maps was published. For a list and description of the early maps that included part or all of Kentucky, see Willard Rouse Jillson, "Early Kentucky Maps," *Register of the Kentucky Historical Society,* XLVII (1949), 226-93; XLVIII (1950), 32-52.

petulant insistence in the Preface to his *Kentucke* that "this performance is not published from lucrative motives." As the owner of more than twelve thousand acres of undeveloped land, the value of which would be enormously enhanced by increased migration, Filson drew his map for the same reason that he wrote his book—to encourage the settlement of Kentucky.

The map and book together, whatever their value to historians today, represent a remarkable piece of promotional literature, including many of the timeworn techniques such as an endorsement by outstanding men. The fanciful rhetoric and the political clichés which characterize much of the writing in the description of Kentucky and in the Boone narrative are neatly balanced by explicit directions on how to secure a land title. Photography, the extremely accommodating ally of modern developers of real estate, is lacking; but in its stead there is a map which is simple and informative as well as stimulating to the imagination of the prospective settler.

Filson may be justly accused of crass economic motives, but there is no doubt that his infatuation with Kentucky was genuine. Compared with his writing about the Illinois country—of which he never got around to drawing a map—his book on Kentucky seems to have been inspired; and it was this same inspiration, sullied as it was by the motive of personal gain, that carried him through the discouragements of drawing and publishing his map. The mood of this strange new land of alternating deciduous woodlands, lush cane, and the great savanna of the "Barrens" had infected him. And if today he knew that he accomplished much more for Kentucky than he did for himself, it is difficult to believe that he would be disappointed.

Although rather crudely drawn, the map possesses an unmistakable charm. In preparing it for publication Filson obviously had one eye on his prospective readers, and particularly on a few highly influential ones. His work lacks many of the colorful embellishments of the maps of an earlier period,[4] but it has several features that are patently designed to attract the attention both of men active in political affairs and of those looking for new homesteads. First, it is prominently "inscribed with the most perfect respect to the Honorable, the Congress of the United States of America, and to his Excell'cy George Washington, late Commander in Chief of their Army." Also, at the top of the map in a plain but conspicuous cartouche Filson expressed his gratitude to Colonel Daniel Boone, Levi Todd, James Harrod, Captain Christopher Greenup, John Cowan, and William Kennedy, who had given him "distinguished assistance in its composition." Finally, by bold type and ingenious pictographs, he set out clearly the most dramatic and attractive features of the landscape: the principal forts that had so recently withstood the fierce Indian assaults; the homes of the pioneers and warriors—Boone, Todd, Shelby, Whitley, Logan, and Johnston—and the rivers, mountains, and "Fine Cane Lands." Also, there were mills, towns, salt springs, roads, and, on the periphery, as reminders of more primitive times, the wigwams of the Shawnee and the Mingo. Clearly marked is the office of Colonel Marshall, the official surveyor, where colonists were required to file their claims for lands. Although the western portion of the district is severely truncated, Filson does include the extensive Green River plains, a tract "which produces no timber and but little Water; mostly Fertile, and covered with excellent Grass and Herbage." Later these lands were to be misleadingly named "The Barrens."

Politically, the territory is divided into three counties: Fayette, Jefferson, and Lincoln; and the map conveys an atmos-

[4] In the history of American cartography, Filson's map belongs at the beginning of a new period—the Period of Emancipation 1780-1820. "Einige Jahre später trennte sich die nordamerikanische Kolonie von ihrer Hauptstadt, und in Jahre 1780 begann eine neue Periode der amerikanische Kartographie—die Periode der Emanzipation (1780-1820)." Leo Bagrow, *Die Geschichte der Kartographie* (Berlin, Safari, 1951), 198.

phere of civilization and progress. Central Kentucky with its network of roads, "some cleared, others not," its dwellings, mills, and towns, appears to be a rather intimate, cozy community. If Filson, who had just come from the cities of Wilmington and Philadelphia, had not had such a strong bias in favor of the rapid settlement of the state, his map would have still portrayed a fertile and romantic land; but doubtless it would have been a more lonely one.

There are several criteria by which this map may be judged: its technical excellence, its accuracy, its historical importance, and its value as a collector's item. Technically, the map is good. It is drawn to scale, ten miles to the inch; there is a clear indication of direction; and there are the customary longitudinal and latitudinal markings that enable the reader to place it on the surface of the earth. Clearly the author was not unskilled in cartography.

When the criterion of accuracy is applied, the map fails to meet it. The most glaring defect is that the district is severely compressed on both the eastern and the western ends. If a copy were mounted on a modern map of the state, drawn to the same scale, all the mountainous territory east of a rough diagonal extending from Kenova, West Virginia, to Middlesboro, Kentucky, would be excluded; and in the west, the meridional line would fall about midway between Henderson and Owensboro on the north and slightly east of Clarksville, Tennessee, in the south. The state at its easternmost point extends about fifty miles beyond the boundary marked by Filson's map, and the Mississippi River boundary falls about one hundred miles to the west of where the map places it. However, since Filson was chiefly interested in the wide rolling meadows of the central part of the territory, it is not at all surprising that his map for this part of the state is much more accurate than it is for the eastern and western extremities.

Less serious errors, but ones that continually plagued the

author, occur in the water courses, which with their myriad branches are tremendously complex in Kentucky. An instance of a gross inaccuracy which Filson inadvertently avoided is shown in his drawing of the Green and Cumberland rivers. The former is entirely within Kentucky, and the upper portion of the latter flows within the present boundaries of the state. If Filson had extended the line between Virginia and North Carolina, which is 36° 30′ north latitude and forms the southern boundary of Kentucky also, it would have been drawn about half a degree above the southern border of the map and would have included only the northern branches of both rivers. Fortunately the line was not drawn.

Despite these errors, however, the map has never received the criticism that has been directed at Filson's literary style. If the conditions under which it was produced are taken into account, the map is amazingly good. It was not drawn from actual surveys entirely, although Filson is supposed to have done considerable surveying along the Ohio River and in central Kentucky. Rather, it was composed in a large measure from secondhand accounts. Furthermore, the speed with which the information was collected would have precluded a careful checking of the facts. In view of these circumstances, it is remarkable that the map is as accurate as it is. This appraisal has been made by a thorough student of Filson's work: "I have often been asked for my opinion as to the accuracy of this early map. The wavy courses for the streams show that it was merely a sketch map. Filson's information came from many people and it was often conflicting. Considering the conditions under which he was laboring, it is a remarkable production, and well answered the purpose for which it was intended, but as a map of Kentucky it is far from accurate."[5]

One is therefore forced to account for the accuracy of the map rather than its errors. And there were two manifest rea-

[5] Thruston, 27-28.

sons why Filson did as well as he did. First, he had excellent sources; the men from whom Filson received his facts were unusually well informed about Kentucky: "It is said of Boone that he was so perfect a woodsman that he could walk up and down a long creek or river and then tell every stream that came into it and designate every peculiarity on both banks. From such men as these Filson got the facts for his history and map, and hence they were wonderful productions for their day."[6]

The second reason why Filson did so well was that he had more than ordinary ability as a surveyor. Proof of this statement was lacking for the admirers of Filson until 1933, when a manuscript map of Wilmington, Delaware,[7] done in his own hand in 1785, came to light. Of his other work—the map of Kentucky and his surveys at Losantiville—no original manuscripts are known to exist.[8] But with the discovery of the map of Wilmington, his ability as a surveyor was established: "the drawing, carefully executed and platted at the scale of 500 feet to the inch, on parchment now yellowed by age and distorted in size, established beyond cavil the outstanding ability and understanding of John Filson as a civil engineer of the abler sort in the year 1785. Herein is explained the ability of the 'pendantic surveyor, school teacher' to produce largely from contemporary descriptions of scouts and travelers so excellent a map as he published of Kentucky in 1784."[9]

[6] Reuben T. Durrett, quoted by Otto A. Rothert, *The Filson Club and Its Activities* (Filson Club *Publications,* no. 32, Louisville, 1922), 7.

[7] The original is preserved in the Delaware Historical Society in Wilmington. Photostat copies are in the Library of Congress and the Filson Club.

[8] Despite the description in the auction catalogue of the library of A. S. Manson, pt. 1, p. 224, title 2114 of a manuscript copy. See G. W. Cole, *A Catalogue of Books Relating to the Discovery and Early History of North and South America Forming a Part of the Library of E. D. Church* (5 vols., New York, Dodd, Mead & Company, 1904), V, 2350-52; and Phillips' comment, *The First Map of Kentucky,* 8-9. Also, a manuscript copy in the Chicago Historical Society was long considered the original draft; but the signature on this copy is sufficiently different from Filson's to cast serious doubt on the claim.

[9] Willard Rouse Jillson, "Filson's Map of Wilmington, Delaware," *Filson Club History Quarterly,* XXVIII (1954), 55-57.

Among his contemporaries, Filson was better known for his map than for anything else that he did;[10] and his ability as a surveyor was recognized not only by the burgesses of Wilmington but also by the men who founded the city of Cincinnati. Today, despite the inaccuracies in the map, its author is regarded as having laid the foundations of Kentucky cartography.[11]

The third criterion by which this map should be judged is its influence in promoting the settlement of Kentucky; but here the evidence is at best indirect. The population of the region increased from 30,000 in 1784,[12] when Filson drew his map, to 100,000 in 1792;[13] but one is compelled to note that Filson's work is a result as well as a cause of this interest in the new West. However, since the publication of the map coincided with the rise of the Kentucky fever—a contagion that spanned the ocean—it is reasonable to suspect that it was a stimulus to this westward migration. This suspicion is strengthened by two contemporary accounts of the caravan that was moving to Kentucky during the years immediately following the publication of Filson's work.

On August 12, 1787, the following item appeared in a Philadelphia newspaper: "We hear that 300 families left Chester County last week, to settle in Kentucke. Their farms were exposed to sale before they sat off, but many of them could not be raised to the value of the taxes due on them."[14] Not only were these Filson's neighbors, but we know also that he was in Chester County about this time, as he was present at the signing of the deed by which he conveyed his farm to his brother Robert on September 8 in the same year.[15] One can

[10] *Dictionary of American Biography,* VI, 382. See also John Hamilton's reminiscences in Chapter VII.

[11] Phillips, 4.

[12] *Kentucke,* 28.

[13] Cotterill, *History of Pioneer Kentucky,* 244.

[14] Philadelphia *Pennsylvania Gazette,* August 12, 1787.

[15] An unrecorded deed in the Chester County Historical Society in West Chester.

think of those conversations which took place in the farmhouses and at the crossroads in the late summer twilight, as the tax-burdened farmers discussed the advantages and disadvantages of removing to Kentucky. There were probably long pauses in their conversations. Many who could not quite muster the courage undoubtedly considered going, so that the number who were interested in their neighbor Filson and his map was in excess of the goodly three hundred who sold their farms.

On August 27, 1789, Lord Dorchester, then Governor General of Canada, wrote Lord Sydney in London that due to the growing importance of the country west of the Appalachian mountains, he was sending him a "plan of the colony of Kentucky."[16] That "plan" was a copy of Filson's map.[17]

Filson would be greatly surprised if he knew that the chief value of his map today is antiquarian, although it would please his vanity to know just how much value of this kind it has.[18] There are nineteen copies of the 1784 engraving extant;[19] and although this number keeps it within the classification of an extremely rare item of Americana, it would have represented a profusion to Filson's first biographer, who had difficulty in finding even one copy.[20] During the nineteenth century the map was so rare—one bibliographer noted it was missing in the copy of *Kentucke* Filson gave to General Washington—that some historians doubted its existence.[21]

Since many rare volumes are lacking maps that are supposed

16 Photostat copy of the letter in the Filson Club.

17 Now in the Public Record Office, London.

18 In January, 1953, a copy of the book and map together sold for six thousand dollars. J. Winston Coleman, Jr., *John Filson, Esq.* (Lexington, Ky., Winburn Press, 1954), 16.

19 Martin F. Schmidt, "Existing Copies of the 1784 Filson Map," *Filson Club History Quarterly,* XXVIII (1954), 55-57.

20 Durrett, *John Filson, the First Historian of Kentucky,* 26.

21 Appleton P. C. Griffin, *A Catalogue of the Washington Collection in the Boston Athenaeum* (Boston, 1897), 80.

to accompany them, it is not unusual for their existence to be doubted. However, it is strange that this doubt should have arisen about Filson's map. Not only was it stated on the title page of his *Kentucke* that there was an accompanying map, but also there was the French reproduction of 1785 in the Paris edition of the book. Furthermore, a catalogue of the Harvard College Library of the year 1831 listed an original copy of the map.[22] It was the rediscovery of the Harvard copy that banished all skepticism about its existence and started the search for additional copies.

The nineteen copies that have been located are classified into "stages" on the basis of the changes that were made in the original engraving.[23] These copies are widely scattered: two are in the hands of private collectors;[24] three are abroad in the British Museum, the Archivo Histórico Nacional, Madrid, and the Colonial Office Library, London, respectively. The others are in university libraries, including Virginia, Harvard, and Michigan; in the Library of Congress; and in historical societies. Drawn in the crude log cabins of the Kentucky wilderness where innumerable hazards threatened its very completion, the map is now preciously handled and securely housed in some of the great repositories of man's cultural achievements.

For Filson all his labor was in vain. He had impetuously designed a grand scheme to make his fortune in Kentucky, and he also expected high recognition for his work. He obtained neither. Had he been less impatient, less prodigal of his restless energy, he might have avoided the envy, the injustice,

22 This copy was from the C. D. Ebeling Collection. "Probably before 1816 a German scholar, Christoph Daniel Ebeling, had collected a library of several thousand books, pamphlets, articles, manuscripts, and maps, relating to America, a collection subsequently acquired by the Harvard College Library." Ralph H. Brown, *Mirror for Americans* (New York, American Geographical Society, 1943), xv.

23 Schmidt.

24 Estate of Frank Deering, Saco, Maine, and Everett D. Graff, Chicago, Illinois.

and the accidents that prevented their realization. If his eye ever wandered from the design of Kentucky to the watermark on the good quality of old laid paper on which it was printed, he would have read the admonition WORK & BE RICH. With this sentiment he was in full accord. But the words were surmounted by the crude design of a plow, an easily overlooked reminder that the road to wealth need be no longer than the furrows on a Chester County farm.

Chapter 7 The Wabash

FOLLOWING the publication of his book and map, Filson stayed on in the East, apparently to see how his work would be received. Interest in his subject was high, and he contemplated a second edition; but when General Washington failed to send an endorsement, the idea was abandoned. There may have been other discouragements too, particularly after the first excitement of seeing his work in print had subsided and he had failed to receive any official recognition for his literary and cartographic efforts.

Although he undoubtedly made frequent visits to nearby Chester County where his relatives lived and where he owned a farm, he spent the winter of 1784-1785 in Philadelphia and Wilmington. His first two letters to General Washington were dated at Philadelphia on November 30 and December 4, and the third one was dated at Wilmington on January 8. It was in the early part of the year 1785 that he drew the map of Wilmington for the "Burgesses and inhabitants" of that town; and one of his former students remembers Filson as his schoolmaster in Wilmington during that year: "I think my memory can bear me back as far as A.D. One thousand seven hundred and eighty-five, at least, in which year I commenced my School Career with a very worthy Scientific Man by the Name of Filson, Who had previously been employed in surveying the Lands of Kentucky, then a Wilderness, and of Which he published a Map. He did not remain long in Wilmington before he returned again to the Western Wilds, and at length fell beneath an Indian's Tomahawk, when on a surveying excursion."[1]

With the coming of spring vivid recollections of Kentucky stirred Filson into making plans to return to the West. In Wilmington he faced the dreary prospect of keeping school for the children of the inhabitants of that city; and at least some of his students were just learning their letters. In Kentucky he had consorted with Daniel Boone; he held in his own name some twelve thousand acres of land; and opportunities for fame and wealth seemed to be unlimited. This time as a man of some reputation and property, he decided to travel in a canvas-top wagon as far as Pittsburgh, where he could embark on one of the flatboats that were already dotting the waters of the Ohio on their way to Limestone [Maysville] and the Falls of the Ohio [Louisville]. However, he had only one horse, and as a consequence he entered into an agreement with John Rice Jones, a young lawyer of Philadelphia, whereby Jones was to furnish "the services of one horse" in a team in return for a passage for himself, his wife Eliza, and his child in Filson's wagon.[2]

Filson's companion for this rough and lonely journey through the forests was a lawyer and a man of learning. Born in Wales in 1759, John Rice Jones reputedly came from a family of high social rank. Following his education at Oxford, he began the practice of law in London. On January 8, 1781, at St. Mary's

[1] John Hamilton (1780-1828), "Some Reminiscences of Wilm't'n and My Youthful Days," manuscript in the Historical Society of Delaware, Wilmington; published in *Delaware History,* I (1946), 88. If the date given for Hamilton's birth is correct, he was only five years of age when he entered Filson's school.

[2] In an expense account Filson kept on the trip, the original of which was in Colonel Durrett's possession when he published his biography of Filson (p. 48).

Chapel in Brecon, Wales, he married Eliza Powell; and three years later he came with his family to Philadelphia. He is reported to have been an excellent mathematician and learned in Greek, Latin, French, Spanish, and Welsh. Later in the West he was to become a prominent man: he was attorney general of the Northwest Territory, a member of the Constitutional Convention of Missouri, and a Justice of the Supreme Court of that state.

Eliza, however, was not to share in the promise the West held for her husband. Three years later she died at Vincennes on the day she bore a son. And Rice, the child who survived the hazards of the trip, met a tragic death at the age of 27. After graduating from Transylvania University in Lexington, he studied medicine in Philadelphia and law in Litchfield, Connecticut. In 1806 he entered politics at Kaskaskia, and on December 7, 1808, he was shot in a political feud. But if the exigencies of frontier travel in the uncertain spring weather allowed any time for reflection, Eliza probably brooded over the memory of her two children left behind in Wales—John, who was dead, and Maria who was too frail to accompany her parents to America—rather than over the unknown events of the future.[3]

The party set out from Wilmington around April 25[4] and arrived in Philadelphia the same day. The next morning they resumed the long overland journey to the Ohio River. The land was beautiful with the first fullness of spring, and soon

[3] W. A. Burt Jones, "John Rice Jones," in Edward G. Mason (ed.), *Early Chicago and Illinois* (Chicago Historical Society *Collections*, no. 4, Chicago, 1890), 230-70. See also J. P. Dunn, Jr., *Indiana* (Boston, Houghton Mifflin Company, 1888), 377.

[4] Colonel Durrett gives the date as the twenty-fifth (*John Filson,* 45). However, in the expense account referred to, Filson enters on April 29 that he received a thermometer from John Rice Jones in Wilmington. It is possible of course that he entered this item a few days after they had begun their journey, when he had time to bring the account up to date.

after taking leave of Filson's relatives in East Fallowfield they were driving through the luxuriant green country of the German farmers in Lancaster. Slowly they reached the wooded uplands, from whose ridges the first foliage of the season could be seen lying in massive and shining waves against the western sun. On through Carlisle, Shippensburg, Ft. Littleton, Bedford, and Ft. Ligonier, they followed the mountain trail, averaging about twelve miles a day. For all the beauty of the landscape the trip was not without its hazards. Eliza and Rice, the child, it appears, withstood the rigors of the 320-mile ride, but both men arrived in Pittsburgh somewhat undone by the adventure—Filson with a bandaged head and Jones ill enough to require drastic medications. Later, in Louisville, Jones told the following anecdote about Filson:

On one occasion, while their wagon was crossing the mountains, Filson, being in front and leading the horses, stooped down to examine a curious rock that had attracted his attention. While thus intent upon his lithological investigation, one of the horses passed on each side of him, and the wagon went over him until the rear axletree was above his head. Filson, then awaking to his situation, threw up his head which, coming in contact with the axletree, pretty nearly made an end of him. He was almost scalped, and made the balance of the way to Pittsburgh with a bandaged head. Filson took the incident goodnaturedly, however, and joked about manufacturing axletrees on a large scale and selling them to the Indians for an improved kind of scalping knives.[5]

And when they arrived in Pittsburgh on May 26, Filson was required to administer to Jones two "vomits" and two "pulverized Peruvian barks," for which he charged a total of nine shillings.[6]

Although he stayed in Pittsburgh only one day, Filson had time to forsee the possibilities of the site and to write another of his sanguine prophecies:

[5] Quoted *ibid.,* 50.

[6] *Ibid.,* 48.

Upon my arrival at pittsburg in May 1785 was agreeably amused with the prospect of that infant City being induced to believe that the time is not far distant when this ample plain will bear the lofty towars and the well regulated Streets Shine with Stately Structures. The Junction of Aleghany & Monongehela rivers nearly at right angles becomes at once the fountain or source of the great Ohio river, which originally was named Belle riviere or fine river by the french, who also named this town fort-duquesne this [manuscript torn] the Vast advantages of the extensive tract of fertile Soil which includes the numerous branches of the affores'd rivers, has that of lying direct on the great high way which at a short period hence, will direct the traveler across the Country to detroit, thus the land and water passages with an extensive prospect of trade proclaims a future City Surpassing most to be found in the interior parts of asiatic Climes.[7]

The rest of the journey to Kentucky was more comfortable. The party abandoned the wagon in Pittsburgh—although they probably took their horses with them—and boarded one of the Kentucky flatboats. At nine o'clock Sunday morning, May 27, they began their voyage down the majestic Ohio. The weather which had been cloudy and showery for the past few days now turned fair and pleasant;[8] and as they proceeded down the Ohio, Filson, using Hutchins' map,[9] studied the landscape and

[7] "A Journal of two Voyages from the falls of the Ohio to Port St. Vincent on Wabash river containing a Variety of remarks and intelligence from that remote quarter by the author of a late publication with a few remarks upon the situation of Pittsburg and the voyage down the rapids," Draper Mss. 10CC35-46; microfilm copy in Princeton University Library. Published as "Two Westward Journeys."

[8] With the thermometer he had purchased from John Rice Jones in Wilmington, Filson kept a record of the temperature: on May 29 the wind was northwest and at ten o'clock in the morning the thermometer stood at 57°. At two o'clock in the afternoon it had risen to 66°, and the next day at the same hour it stood at 70°. From a very sketchy diary commencing May 18, apparently some rough notes from which Filson wrote his "A Journal of Two Voyages." Draper Mss. 10CC1-34, p. 31.

[9] This map of the Ohio country was prepared in 1764 by Thomas Hutchins. A more elaborate edition was published in 1775. See *A Topographical Description of Virginia, Pennsylvania, Maryland and North Carolina* (London, J. Almon, 1778).

the location of the forts. The bewitching beauty of an Ohio valley spring did not distract him from practical considerations, and when he reached the mouth of the Great Kanawha, he was

> induced at this place to take observations with an instrum't in order to form a plan and ascertain the breadth of boath rivers was informed that about 90 miles up Kenhawa was a great rapid Conclude that a portage there will be necessary to assist the navigation above and below, and believe this place will be direct in the road that may lead from Phil'a. to the nearest part of the Kentucke country and So on in the straighest direction that possible Can be to the falls of Ohio and may probably afford a better road than any heretofore traveled between those places and Shorten the distance at least 200 miles.[10]

Much farther on, after the Ohio had turned west and had flowed in that direction for something like a hundred miles, Filson observed the growing and important "port" of Limestone, where immigrants disembarked to settle inland on the famous limestone plateau that forms central Kentucky. From there on, the landscape was less rugged and the river had reached almost its maximum breadth and depth, with only the danger of the rapids at the Falls to keep it from being an ideal waterway. Always impressed with the advantage of superior routes of trade, this prophet of the West predicted that Louisville, which had then been established for about ten years, "is probably the foundation of one of the greatest cities on earth."

On June 10 the boat was moored at the mouth of Beargrass Creek,[11] and Filson was once again in Kentucky. His first recorded act certainly was not performed in the grand manner—he sued John Rice Jones for his share of the expenses of the trip.[12] In good schoolmasterly fashion Filson had kept an accurate account of the amounts paid out by both parties and found that Jones owed him seven pounds, seventeen shillings,

[10] Draper Mss. 10CC35-46; "Two Westward Journeys," 323.

[11] Durrett, *John Filson,* 47.

[12] *Ibid.,* 49.

and seven pence.[13] When Jones did not pay promptly, Filson resorted to legal means to force the satisfaction of the debt, and before Squire Richard Terrell he obtained a judgment for the amount. Jones, however, had no property that was subject to attachment. What followed is told in one of the anecdotes that have contrived to make Filson a somewhat ludicrous character. Keeping a close and stubborn watch on the premises of the defendant, he thought one day that Jones had acquired a cow. Proceeding immediately to Squire Alexander Breckinridge, Filson obtained an attachment and hurriedly had

[13] John Rice Jones Dr. To John Filson

		S	D
April 30, 1785. To cash paid for his freight and passage from Philadelphia to Wilmington	0	15	0
For keeping his horse before our procedure on our journey 15 days,	0	15	0
May 26. His passage in the wagon to Pittsburgh; his wife and child's passage to Pittsburgh	3	7	6
Carriage of 217 lbs at 85s pr C	4	17	7
Two books and two maps of mine in Pittsburgh	0	15	0
Cash in pay for bread and butter in do,	0	6	0
Two vomits	0	4	0
Pulverized Peruvian barks at twice	0	5	0
Cash for his horse feed after arrival in Pittsburgh	0	1	2
Removing his property from the town in Pittsburgh on board the boat	0	5	0
Pennsylvania currency	11	11	3
Equal to do. in Virginia currency (not to be confused with depreciated Ca. currency)	9	5	0
June 10. To one of my maps in Louisville		5	
	9	10	0
	1	12	5
Balance due in Virginia currency	7	17	7

Contra Cr.

Recd. from John Rice Jones the services of his horse in my team to Pittsburgh in consequence of an agreement in Wilmington with him on act. of his passage in the wagon.

		S	D
April 29, 1785. Recd from him in Wilmington one thermometer and case,	0	19	0
One Book of Carver's Travels,	0	9	0
One Book of Gibson's surveying	0	12	0
Pennsylvania currency	2	0	6
Equal do. in Virginia currency	1	12	5

it executed by Deputy Sheriff Reuben Eastin. It was to Filson's embarrassment that the cow was discovered to be a roving and unruly bull that had strayed into Jones' field.

Filson was disgusted by this episode and gave up all attempts to collect the money. Furthermore, he was busy making preparations for another journey, this time to the Illinois country, which was then on the minds of the Kentuckians. In 1778 George Rogers Clark had explored the Old Northwest and had claimed the territory for Virginia. Finding it difficult to establish control over the remote settlements on the Wabash and hoping to guarantee the title to her lands southeast of the Ohio, Virginia ceded the territory to the national government in 1784.[14] Some of Clark's men liked the territory around Post St. Vincent well enough to want to return. Consequently, between 1778 and 1787 about four hundred Americans, mostly Kentuckians, had migrated to this far-western outpost of American civilization.[15]

On July 14 Filson with some unknown companions set out in a canoe down the Ohio. Seven days later they reached the mouth of the Wabash and from there took eleven days to reach Post St. Vincent. As was his custom, the curious Filson kept a journal en route, perhaps with a view to publishing another book about the West:

> I frequently went on shore for discoveries, and found the Soil amazingly fertile observed that honey Suckles were exceeding plenty, discovered the Catolopy [catalpa] tree of large growth the Cotton [cottonwood] tree as frequent as any other Species, and a tree of large growth, of which kind I have not Seen before of Since but doubtless possessing rare & Valuable qualities for from its trunk proceeded a gum of aromatic, and on its branches multitude of

14 The negotiations for the cession of these western lands had begun in 1781. Clarence Edwin Carter (ed.), *The Territorial Papers of the United States* (20 vols. to date, Washington, Department of State, 1934-), II, 6-9.

15 Letter from Brigadier General Harmar to the Secretary of War, dated at Post Vincennes, August 7, 1787. William Henry Smith (ed.), *The St. Clair Papers* (2 vols., Cincinnati, R. Clarke & Co., 1882), 26-30.

Small balls which were then green but afforded the most delicious Smell that I ever experienced in nature way so exquisite was the effluvia that I really conceived a respiral healing and pleasure perhaps a Curious enquiry of the Valuable qualities of the tree may yet be interesting to mankind.[16]

Although the Indians were beginning to show signs of renewed hostility to the Americans, Filson's party was not attacked; and along the way they exchanged flour, salt, and tobacco for meat, fish, and fowl. The nearest they came to an unpleasant encounter is described in the journal:

one day a number of their pirouges hove in Sight & according to their Custom a gun was fired to know whether we were friends or foes, as it appears that answering with a gun is a mark of friendship. We being unacquainted with this fired no gun, and observed the indians to hurry on Shore requiring us to Come to them which we answered by Signs desiring them to Come to us; they Complied and advancing to us, we met them with every mark of good nature and proposed to present them with some of our provisions, they appeared pleased except one and the Sign being given for all to move on Shore, upon landing, the indian who appeared Sour and by his ornaments might be Suposed to be a prince drew out a large knife and advanced up to one of our Compans (who was no ways Suspicious) in a resolute manner as if a mortal stab might be the Consequence, but all on a Sudden from what Cause may be uncertain he turned his weapon aside and took him by the hand in a friendly manner, this might be induced to by observing one of us (a good woodsman) & acquainted with indian Customs to keep his gun in order for immediate execution; however the Scene ended in friendship & we gave them Chearfully & bountifully & departed.[17]

Upon arriving at Post St. Vincent, Filson was impressed with the hospitality of the French, and in characteristic fashion he immediately set about interrogating the inhabitants about the history of the town, how it was governed, its advantages as a

[16] Draper Mss. 10CC35-46. Bond (ed.), "Two Westward Journeys," 325, believes this tree was the juniper.

[17] Draper Mss. 10CC35-46; "Two Westward Journeys," 326.

trading center, and the customs of the people. He must have spent the few days he was there in a continuous round of interviews, collecting and recording with some inaccuracies and not much discrimination a great deal of data about the Post.

At nine o'clock on the morning of August 11 he started back to Louisville[18] with the intention of returning on a trading mission. This time he took the much shorter overland route. Accompanying him were Captains Buckley and Pierrault and four guides. It took him nine days to arrive at Louisville, where he immediately began making plans to return, ostensibly in order to engage in some form of trading, probably in furs.

There were several reasons why Filson wanted to return to Post St. Vincent. Apparently he had acquired a love of wandering on the frontiers and the Illinois country offered him all the stimulation of a new settlement. Probably, too, he was planning to write another book, although he never became so enthusiastic about the future of this region as he had about Kentucky. A third reason was his interest in acquiring more land that might someday become valuable. And finally, he was planning to engage in some form of trade, an enterprise that required substantial capital.[19] So eager was he for money that on October 14, 1785, he gave a bond for a deed to his farm in Chester County to Daniel Henry, a merchant of Louisville. The next day he received from Henry 735 pounds "lawful money of Pennsylvania currency,"[20] the price agreed upon for the 240 acres on the Brandywine that he had inherited from his thrifty father. Henry took the unusual precaution of having the bond signed by six witnesses in addition to the clerk, a fact that could reflect on Filson's reputation for hon-

18 Draper Mss. 10CCb; microfilm copy in the Princeton University Library.

19 Leonard Clinton Helderman, "The Northwest Expedition of George Rogers Clark 1786-87," *Mississippi Valley Historical Review,* XXV (1937-1938), 317-34. "He [Filson] had come hither to this 'remote and dangerous part' to spend the winter, keep a sharp eye out for an honest penny in the fur trade and establish himself as a first settler with more lands to patent" (p. 317).

20 Minute Book No. 1, p. 43, Jefferson County, Louisville, Kentucky. Quoted in full in Durrett, *John Filson,* 44, 55.

"Squire Boone Crossing the Mountains with Supplies for His Brother Daniel Encamped in the Wilds of Kentucky," a painting by William Ranney owned by the J. B. Speed Art Museum, Louisville.

esty. However, for other reasons also the grantee was justified in demanding extraordinary proof of his right to the deed: Filson was wandering about on hazardous jaunts and Henry foresaw the difficulties involved if he ever had to prove his claim alone in faraway Chester County.

It was from the wording of this bond that Colonel Durrett assumed that Filson had given up his citizenship in Pennsylvania: "Know all men by these presents, that John Filson, of Jefferson County, and Commonwealth of Virginia . . ." However, as later records show, this statement was merely a *descriptio personae* rather than an indication of Filson's legal residence.

Filson arrived at Post St. Vincent for the second time about Christmas, which the farmers along the Brandywine were celebrating with Presbyterian decorum. It is hardly conceivable that he was not afflicted with a deep nostalgia when he contemplated his situation in the rough and bawdy frontier town. Conditions since his last visit had altered considerably: "a hovering Cloud pregnant with innumerable evil was obvious over Post St Vincent, the indians also began to quarrel with the americans and frequent murders ensued."[21]

The Indians were becoming increasingly hostile toward the Americans, and the ill-feeling between the Americans and the French had been aggravated by the "magisteril ordinance prohibiting the Sail of the noxious Juices." A few days after he arrived, Filson found himself the butt of another, and exceedingly grim, frontier prank: "for a few days after I was Settled there a Frenchman who lived near me was murdered and laid at my door in the night, perhaps the perpetrator of this horrid action might have Some design as I was a Stranger, but the better sort of people being so prejudiced in my favor it rather turned out to my advantage."[22] According to one account the

21 Draper Mss. 10CC35-46; "Two Westward Journeys," 330.

22 *Ibid.* See also, George R. Wilson and Gayle Thornbrough, *The Buffalo Trace* (Indiana Historical Society *Publications,* vol. 15, no. 2, Indianapolis, 1946), 195.

Frenchman had been killed on New Year's night in a drunken orgy with the Indians, and some wags placed the corpse at Filson's door.[23] He, however, failed to see any humor in the situation, a not unusual reaction. Also, the Calvinist in Filson revolted at the debauchery that was habitual at the Post: "No people on earth live more chearfully than the people of this place balls and reveling take their nightly round, Vice and profanity become Common and habitual, the Court became in Some measure the ridicule of the people by a prostitution of their Characters to Gambling & Luxury."[24]

Added to the general gloom of the situation was the fact that Filson was having some kind of financial difficulty. On December 30 he executed a note to John Brown, a young lawyer in Louisville: "I acknowledge myself indebted to John Brown the amount of sixty-one dollars or sixty-one pounds of beaver, which I promise to pay to him upon demand next spring either at Post St. Vincent or Falls of Ohio. Witness my hand this 30th day of Decr., Anno Domini 1785. Testes, John Adams."[25] Whether this debt was for professional services—it was a rather large sum for that—or whether it was a business obligation we do not know. The mention of beaver furs, although they might have been merely a medium of exchange, arouses a suspicion that Filson was engaging in the fur trade and not prospering at it. Another anecdote about his guilelessness adds support to this theory. A tale was told that on one occasion a trapper tried to sell Filson some muskrat skins, but he replied that he was interested only in beavers. The trapper, sensing Filson's innocence in such matters, removed the tails from the muskrat skins and brought them back to Filson as young beavers, the most valuable of all. Filson is reported to have paid a high price for the skins and to have lost considerably in the transaction.

Filson was active in affairs at the Post. The situation there

23 Durrett, *John Filson,* 55.

24 Draper Mss. 10CC35-46; "Two Westward Journeys," 330.

25 Quoted from Durrett, who had the original. *John Filson,* 53.

was perilous for the inhabitants and was rapidly growing worse; the Indians, resenting the continuing encroachment of the Americans, were organizing against them.[26] On March 16, 1786, Filson joined with the Americans in a petition to George Rogers Clark, then in Kentucky, to march again to the Wabash to relieve the inhabitants.[27] Again on June 1, the day he left the Post, Filson drafted a petition to the Congress of the United States on behalf of the American families in the town, pleading for military protection, regular government, and particularly for some security for the land titles of the Americans:

The representation and petition of the subscribers, inhabitants of Post St. Vincent, in the County of Illinois, most humbly sheweth. That your Petitioners, having lately emigrated to this district, expecting to enjoy the blessings of peace and property, and as faithful subjects to the United States, beg leave to represent, that searching for a fertile soil on the banks of the Wabash river, was invited by the bounties of nature to settle our families here, to promote our happiness, being welcome by the french inhabitants, we obtained lotts in town and lands in the Country, by virtue of an office established here by Lieut. Govr. Todd, but many doubts have arisen amongst us concerning their validity, knowing that Mr. Todds appointment was at an unsettled period and probably invested with no powers or instructions to institute a land office. The french pretend to Claim a District of twelve leagues square including the town, but we are not confirmed that they have the right to such territory, neither are they But our disappointment in procuring property for our families, is at present the smallest evil we are involved in, being surrounded and invested with hostile savages, whose antipathy to americans, exposing daily to danger and frequent death, this our calamitous situation we expect wil be fully & truely explained to you by our truths . . . we therefore look up to you the supreme authority of the United States, as the guardians of our lives, liberty, and property, humbly praying that you will take us under your serious consideration & patronage; that you will of your clemency be pleased to ordain a permanent land office here,

26 "Defeat on the Wabash," 188-99. See also, Leonard Clinton Helderman, "Danger on the Wabash: Vincennes Letters of 1786," *Indiana Magazine of History,* XXXIV (1938), 456-58.

27 Draper Mss. 53J23; published in Helderman, "Danger on the Wabash."

for the purpose of obtaining valid rights to lands, under the conduct of proper gentlemen, and considering us as first settlers, labouring under innumerable losses and Disadvantages, be pleased to grant such portions of land for each settler as may in some measure compensate for our present pressing circumstances; Being now without order, law or government by any executive, which adds greatly to our distressed situation, we humbly pray that you will appoint a regular government in this place and territory, under the conduct of good men, as the Commandant and Magistracy of this place have resigned & refused to act on account of disobdeince in the people; and also we pray that a strong garrison may be established here, for a support to the dignity of the Civil power, and a defense against imperious hostile savages. If your honorable body will be pleased to order affairs in this place, we humbly conceive that the banks of the Wabash would soon be inhabited by numerous valuable subjects; but should so valuable an acquisition of settlement and our distressed situation, be so unhappy as not to merit your attention, we must experience destruction which will totally prevent an emigration, which lately appeared the most promising and interesting, but this is most distant from our hopes and expectations; we your petitioners therefore hopeing to receive encouragement from your clemency, pray that this may have a gracious acceptance, and as in duty bound your supplinats must ever esteem you an inestimable blessing to them, and perpetually and gratefully remember your favours.
Dated June 1, 1786[28]

On the same day on which he had written the petition for the inhabitants, Filson with three companions started for the Falls of the Ohio in a pirogue, the beginning of a memorable frontier journey. In Filson's own words the elements that night were foreboding: "the night was gloomy, Clouds and double darkness veil'd the skies, the descending moisture appeared to mourn our approaching fate."[29] Two of his men were in a stupor, having partaken too freely of the "noxious juices," and were unable to help with the rowing. Apprehensive of Indian attacks, Filson was impatient to row as far as possible before

[28] Draper Mss. 53J31; published in Helderman, "Danger on the Wabash," 457-58.

[29] Draper Mss. 10CCc 22 pages; published in Helderman, "Defeat on the Wabash," 189.

the daybreak, but it came, unwelcomed, when they were about twelve leagues below the Post. As soon as they had eaten breakfast in the boat, they were fiercely attacked by Indians. Filson's hat was shot through, a fact that seemed to unnerve him less than the bloodcurdling war whoops of the savages. After landing on the shore, the men fled, but Filson crept under a cover of cane and wild nettles, where he watched the red warriors landing in eager pursuit. The foliage was wet, and Filson observed that where it had yielded to his steps, it did not recover. Fearing that the "sagacious" savages would soon find him, he started in crafty flight, using many "windings and turnings": "In flight I oft turned my eyes from behind some ancient friendly tree, to view some bloodthirsty savage, in full chase, with his terrible right arm, to lodge me in the land of silence."[30]

After two hours of desperate but successful wandering, Filson stealthily came back to the spot where he had landed, and there he found his trunks unmolested but the liquor gone, a fact that may account for the Indians' abandoning the chase. Two of his men had been scalped, and the third was badly shaken with fright. Filson immediately crossed the river on an improvised raft and barely escaped drowning; but an even more melancholy prospect faced him—he had to make his way back to the Post through the dense, savage-infested wilderness:

The day began to decline, and heavy showers fell; the briers and thorns tore my cloathes, and my flesh experienced the most excrutiating pain, from their repeated assaults, and the invenomed nettles. Hunger now began to rage. I felt languid and my burthen increased with wet. Those lines in Homer came lively

> Oh friends a thousand ways frail mortals lead
> To the cold tomb, and dreadful all to tread;
> But dreadful most, when by a slow decay
> Pale hunger wastes the manly strength away.[31]

The next day, near complete exhaustion, he reached the Post,

[30] *Ibid.,* 190.
[31] *Ibid.,* 191. *The Odyssey* (Pope trans.), bk. 12, ll. 341-44.

where he lodged with Colonel John Small,[32] who was generally regarded as the leader of the Americans there.

Despite the insistence of his friends not to expose himself again to the dangers of a trip to Kentucky, Filson was determined to leave the Post. Two reasons he gave for his decision: the "unhappy contentions" between the Americans and the French, aggravated by the relations existing between the Americans and the savages; and a "desire to see my friends, and native soil." So ten days later, on June 12, he and a "hardy woodsman" left by an overland route at night, when the moon shone with "an agreeable lustre." Seven painful days later he arrived at the Falls of the Ohio, bearing the petition to Congress and a letter from Colonel Small to General Clark, stating that unless Clark sent aid, the inhabitants of the Post would be destroyed.[33]

The Indian troubles along the Wabash increased in intensity during the summer, and after an abortive attempt by a volunteer force from Kentucky to relieve the inhabitants of the Post, Clark at last marched into the territory about the middle of September. The results of this expedition were far from decisive and the Americans along the Wabash remained uneasy. Filson, however, was no longer concerned. By early September, while the excessive heat of that summer continued,[34] he was on horseback, riding along the Wilderness Road on his way back to Chester County.

32 Colonel Small was later mentioned in Filson's will as his attorney for his property in Vincennes.

33 Draper Mss. 53J32.

34 Supplies for Clark's army were delayed during the latter part of September by the low stage of the Wabash and much of the food was spoiled by the excessive heat. See Helderman, "The Northwest Expedition of Clark," 327.

Chapter 8 Schoolmaster

TWO ROUTES there were from the Falls of the Ohio to Philadelphia. One of these was by way of the Ohio River as far as Pittsburgh and then across the mountains on the upper Pennsylvania trail. The second was the famous Wilderness Road that led southeastward to the Cumberland Gap and from there northward through the Valley of Virginia. Filson had noted it on his map as "The Road from the Old Settlements in Virginia to Kentucky thro' the Great Wilderness." Resistless tides of immigration were following it westward—

> Some to endure, and many to quail
> Some to conquer, and many to fail
> Toiling over the Wilderness Trail;[1]

but it was also the more practical route for the occasional eastward traveler. It was possible to make one's way upstream to Pittsburgh, but the trip was difficult and tedious; furthermore, on the water one was helplessly exposed in the event of an Indian attack. After his harrowing "defeat" on the Wabash, it is not surprising that Filson chose the all-land route.

As Filson was ready to leave Louisville another misfortune occurred: his horse ran away. But he soon obtained another and by September 9 he had ridden as far as Danville, where he wrote his creditor, John Brown: "I was Delayed, at Louisville by my Creature that left me. I hear you are gone to Cumberland but if ever you receive this, I request you to trade my note which will be equal to Cash in the neighbourhood of Harrod's Station which I Can ans. at my return. Mr. Geo. Caldwell will be a likely man to trade with you, I have but little Money, but my will is good, therefore you will excuse me."[2] On the back of this letter he wrote: "I expect to return before Christmas, farewell my friend adeiu."

Leaving Danville, Filson began a horseback journey of almost eight hundred miles. Riding through dense and solitary forests, where the rays of the autumn sun bronzed in varied patterns the carpet of leaves by day, and where by night his campfire illumined the overhanging boughs, this lonely and quixotic schoolmaster made a fragile silhouette against the primeval wilderness. He was not a woodsman like Boone, nor did he possess Boone's temperament. In the terrifying loneliness of the nights he must have been incalculably miserable. The call of a bird, the mournful hoot of an owl, or the occasional crash of a falling branch would remind him of the strategems of hostile Indians; and his recent experiences on his way back from Post St. Vincent certainly must have heightened his vivid imagination.

The names on this land of Appalachia give eloquent testimony to the character of the country through which Filson rode:[3] Logan's Station, the Crab Orchard, the Ford on Rockcastle River, Hazel Patch, Laurel Run, Raccoon Spring, Stinking Creek, Fork of Cumberland River, Martin's Cabins, Block House, Head of Holston, Stone Mill, Forks of the Road, Patterson's on Roanoke, Botetourt Court House, the Shenandoah, Winchester, York, Lancaster, and finally, familiar Fallowfield.

[1] Winston Churchill, *The Crossing* (New York, Macmillan Company, 1904), 81.

[2] Facsimile in Durrett, *John Filson,* facing p. 72.

[3] In Thomas Speed, *The Wilderness Road* (Filson Club *Publications,* no. 2, Louisville, 1886), there are several contemporary accounts by early immigrants in Kentucky who came this way.

These sparsely settled mountains were desolate enough at best; but to Filson, who was penniless and homesick, the journey must have been dreary indeed.

Weary and travel-stained, Filson arrived home sometime before November 7, for on that date he borrowed eight pounds in gold and silver from David Park in Wilmington.[4] Also, within the month he made his will. While it is possible that amid the peace and plenty of Chester County he had occasion to reflect upon the uncertainty of human life on the frontier from which he had just come and to which he would soon return, it is likely also that the will was made at the suggestion of his brother Robert. As later events show, Robert was bearing a heavy responsibility for John's debts; and it is not surprising that he was made the sole legatee of all Filson's lands in Kentucky, as well as the property and notes due at Post St. Vincent.[5]

We do not know whether Filson made good his promise to return to Kentucky by Christmas or not. The year 1787 is an obscure one in his life. Dim records of debts, lawsuits, and wanderings throw a pale and cheerless light on his activities. In February of the previous year, while he was at Post St. Vincent, Filson through his attorney had sued John K. Simpson of Stanford for an undetermined sum and had won the suit.[6] The next year he was involved in a series of court actions. At Harrodsburg or Lexington he sued John Morrison for a debt of sixteen livres and eight sous that had been contracted at Post St. Vincent.[7] When Morrison, who could not be found

[4] Original note in the Clarke Collection, Ohio Historical and Philosophical Society, Cincinnati.

[5] This will was dated November 21, 1786, and witnessed by Mary Hartt and Bryan McCune. See Wilson, "John Filson in Pennsylvania," 182.

[6] February Court, Lincoln County, Stanford, Kentucky.

[7] The original record of this action has not been found. The author has relied on Colonel Durrett's account, *John Filson*, 70. The court records of Fayette County, in which this suit was filed, are incomplete. Microfilm copies of those extant are in the University of Kentucky Library, but they contain no reference

at the time of the litigation, was reported to be in the vicinity of Harrodsburg, Filson literally ordered Robert Patterson, the sheriff, to execute the judgment: "You must execute this immediately. The man is near Harrodsburg he is lately from Post St. Vincent a middle aged man. by strict enquiry you will hear of him. Delay no time Spare no search for him."[8] Thus the impatient schoolmaster addressed the high sheriff of Fayette County.

Meanwhile, Filson was being sued. He had failed to pay his debt of sixty-one dollars to John Brown. Consequently, in September of 1787, while Filson was in Chester County, Brown brought suit in Louisville to collect the debt.[9] When he obtained judgment, he could find no property of Filson's to attach—none but an old sickle. Presumably Filson held title to some twelve thousand acres of land in Fayette County and bonds for fifteen thousand acres in Jefferson County,[10] but the only personal property he owned in Kentucky was an old-fashioned reaping hook.

Sometime during the year, probably in the late summer, Filson made another trip to Chester County. On September 7 he was present when he sold his farm to his brother Robert—the same farm he had deeded by bond to Daniel Henry in Louisville in the fall of 1785—and he received "three hundred pounds Specie" in payment.[11] By this time he felt under no obligation to honor his bond to Henry, because the latter had failed to make good a title to a tract of land in Maryland which had been assigned to Filson. This transaction was a tangled

---

to Filson. There is, however, an original list of accounts owed Filson by the residents of Vincennes in the Clarke Collection, Ohio Historical and Philosophical Society Library, Cincinnati, in which the name of John Morrison is listed.

8 Durrett, *John Filson,* 70, copied verbatim from the original.

9 Again the author is forced to rely on Durrett, who had the original records. *Ibid.,* 78.

10 See will of John Filson in Wilson, 182.

11 Unrecorded deed in the Chester County Historical Society, West Chester, Pennsylvania.

one in which it appears that Daniel Henry had agreed under the penalty of two thousand pounds to make a "clear and indisputable title" to 167 acres on Seneca Creek in Maryland to Squire Boone, a brother of Daniel. Boone in turn assigned this land to Filson, but neither was able to get a clear title from Henry. This matter was the chief subject of a letter Filson wrote his brother from Redstone Old Fort on November 20, 1787, while on his way back to Kentucky for the third and last time:

Dr. Brother

The enclosed article was assigned to me yesterday You will see it is a personal agreement wherein Daniel Henry is bound under the penal sum of 2000 pounds to make a Clear indisputable title to Squire Boone his heirs or assigns by the 7th day of September 1786, and to put him or assigns into possession when required You will see that the purchase money by a list of bonds on the backside was 500 pounds Virginia Currency, which bonds were assigned to him and thereby he acknowledges payment, he never has made a deed for said land nor ever Can, I am Certain, but to render him inexcusable, as soon as you receive this, go down to Baltimore as you have a power of attorney and the articles —— to you from me and by that authority demand before Ligget and Some others a deed & possession of the premises, and payment of his note of 20 pounds which you have, as it Cannot be legally recovered from Boone he being gone among the Savages—also demand of him the rents he may have rec'd, if Joseph Could avoid paying him it would be well, but I Suppose he has his note. You will know how to manage him, have your evidences qualified and offer him to exchange bonds with him and Clear all matters, but I fear he will assign my bond away, or will send it after me to Kentucke in that Case we shall have a Suit in law & I shall fling him, but you must Collect the testimonies of your demanded possession, and assign this article back to me and enfold all Safely in a letter and Send it by Mr. Cowan next spring, with your instructions; as this writing is worth 200 pounds Currency be Careful of it. In exchangeing bonds, Henry may plead that I rec'd 35 pounds worth of goods but as this affair Cost me two Journeys to pennsylvania & much trouble I make him no Allowance, Save to deliver him up his note and,—receipts of acquittance & not otherwise, but if he will not settle, this note an attested acc't of the rent must be Sent to me and I Shall balance with him You will not fail, and when in Baltimore enquire of Robert Dunn if he Sold any books & maps as I left 15 of each with him & also of Rich'd ——. You will not fail to come out to Cousin Bobs[12] for the horses the first week in march and hire a pack horse for his son as I mentioned in my former letter, by Mr. ——. You will not fail to Send me what I desired if possible. I am tolerably hapy & in good health & this moment I step on board to sail down to Kentucke fine water & Weather and the river crowded with boats My love to Mr. Hartt & Daughter & all enquiring friends. I hope you will be Content and enjoy yourself until I return & mind my instructions Concerning affairs I hope you are in possession of health I wish you to inform me particularly how you are and when you would wish my return. Joseph shall go home when Circumstances admit toward Spring or fall, I remain Dr. Brother yrs. unalterably

John Filson[13]

Accompanying this letter were the documents in question and a power of attorney for Robert Filson. Apparently Daniel Henry never gave Filson a clear title to the land, for in April of the next year Filson published the following notice:

Kentucky Gazette, April 19, 1788

Whereas Daniel Henry, of Baltimore, did in October, 1785, at the falls of Ohio, obtain a bond from me for the conveyance of a certain tract of Land in Pennsylvania: This is to forewarn all persons from taking an assignment of said bond, the same caution I have given the Maryland Gazette: for I am determined not to comply therewith; as I have in my possession a bond of his for conveyance of a tract of land in Maryland of equal value, which land I am convinced he has lost, and consequently his conveyance to me impossible.

John Filson[14]

12 Robert *Ph*ilson, Senior, and Robert Philson, Junior, were in Berkeley Court, Virginia, during the Revolution. Anne Waller Reddy, *West Virginia Revolutionary Ancestors* (Washington, Model Printing Company, 1930), 62.

13 Original letters and power of attorney in the Clarke Collection, Ohio Historical and Philosophical Society, Cincinnati.

14 Copied in C. Frank Dunn, "John Filson and Transylvania Seminary," *Register of the Kentucky Historical Society,* XLV (1947), 324-34.

When Filson returned to Kentucky about December 1, he found the residents of Lexington interested in two subjects: statehood and education. Both interests indicated how rapidly civilization was moving into the tramontane region. Only four years earlier, when Filson made his first visit to Kentucky, the inhabitants who had survived the Indian wars were still dazed by the enormity of the sacrifice required for the sheer colonization of this uninhabited land. But now, although the Indians were still threatening, the Kentuckians had enough leisure and security to concern themselves with political and educational institutions.

As early as 1780 the Virginia legislature had provided for a seminary of learning in the new and bloody county of Kentucky; and in 1783 it was chartered as Transylvania Seminary.[15] However, not until 1794 was this institution any more than a common grammar school, whose fortunes fluctuated with the exigencies of frontier life. Seven of the infant seminary's trustees and friends were killed by the Indians.[16]

Transylvania was a state institution, but even before it was established, it became entangled in a conflict between orthodox Christianity and "infidelity," a conflict that was in fact a struggle between Presbyterianism and various forms of religious liberalism—Arianism, Socinianism, Unitarianism, and Deism. Among the orthodox Christians, the Presbyterians were the ones most interested in education, and the majority of their clergy in Kentucky were extremely strict in their adherence to Calvinism. The Episcopalians by comparison were theological liberals, but politically they were still under the shadow of Toryism. The Methodists and Baptists—the former Arminian and emotional, and the latter Calvinistic and evangelistic—were more concerned with personal religious experience than

15 Hening (ed.), *Statutes at Large*, XI, 286.

16 For the history of Transylvania University, see Robert M. Peter, *Transylvania University*, (Filson Club *Publications*, no. 11, Louisville, 1896); Niels Henry Sonne, *Liberal Kentucky, 1780-1828* (New York, Columbia University Press, 1939); and Lewis, *History of Higher Education in Kentucky*, 35-100.

with higher education. The battle for the religious control of state education thereore resolved itself into a struggle between the Presbyterians and those of Unitarian and deistic views.[17]

The act by which Transylvania Seminary was created provided that the state should endow academies as "nursery schools" for the seminary.[18] These like the seminary were slow in being established, and by the summer of 1787 the people of Lexington were clamoring for schools of secondary rank. As a consequence a number of private academies were started in that year and the next. The first school in Lexington had opened in 1780 with John McKinney as teacher; he later acquired the sobriquet "Wildcat" as the result of a fierce battle with a stray wildcat in his classroom.[19] The second teacher was probably John Filson, although one wonders how much time he had for teaching during his first visit in 1783-1784. As a consequence of the demand for academies, they began springing up during the latter part of 1787. Typical of these early academies is the one opened by Elijah Craig:

> Notice is hereby given, that on Monday the 28th of January next, a school will be opened by Messrs. Jones & Worley, at the royal spring in Lebanon town, Fayette county, where a commodious house, sufficient to contain fifty or sixty scholars, will be prepared. They will teach the Latin and Greek languages, together with such

[17] The liberals finally lost influence, but not until after the religious climate of Kentucky had changed. Before 1800 Transylvania had an Episcopalian, James Moore, and a Unitarian, Harry Toulmin, for presidents; and during its most famous period—1818-1827—Horace Holley, a Unitarian minister, was president. The majority of the early inhabitants of Kentucky were not sectarian minded. As late as 1800, when the population of the state was 220,955, only 10,000 belonged to any church. Sonne, 13. After the turn of the century and the great revivals, the religious character of the population changed. More people belonged to church, and out of the conflicting religious movements—Calvinism, Liberalism, and Revivalism—many fragments had splintered off the ecclesiastical bodies. Liberalism lost out as a separate force, but it remains as a component in the only major indigenous American denomination—the Disciples of Christ—now in control of Transylvania College.

[18] Hening (ed.), *Statutes at Large,* XI, 286, sec. 3.

[19] Collins, *History of Kentucky,* II, 225-26.

branches of the sciences as are usually taught in the public seminaries, at twenty-five shillings a quarter for each scholar, one half to be paid in cash, the other in produce at cash price. There will be a vacation of a month in the spring and another in the fall, at the close of which, it is expected that such payments as are due in cash, will be made. For diet, washing and house-room, for a year, each scholar pays three pounds in cash, or five hundred weight of pork on entrance, and three pounds cash on the beginning of the third quarter. It is desired that as many as can would furnish themselves with beds; such as cannot may be provided for here to the number of eight or ten boys, at thirty-five shillings a year for each bed.

Elijah Craig

N.B. It would be proper for each boy to have his sheets, shirts, stockings, etc. marked to prevent mistakes.
Lebanon, December 27, 1787.[20]

Other schools that opened about the same time were the Lexington Grammar School, with Isaac Wilson, formerly a professor in Philadelphia College, teaching Latin, Greek, and science;[21] Ebenezer Brooks' school in Jessamine County; and James Priestly's Salem Academy at Bardstown.[22]

The controversy about the place of sectarian religion in the curriculum extended to secondary education. In the columns of the *Kentucky Gazette* a whole spate of articles continued a discussion, which was bitter and satirical. A paper signed "Catholicus" dismissed the Jeffersonian idea that morals be taught without theology[23] as a policy that might eliminate sectarian jealousy, but one which would also tend to eradicate the Christian religion. Therefore, diversity of sectarian views should be presented to students. "Paddy Money-Man" and "A

20 Lexington *Kentucky Gazette,* December 27, 1787; copied in Collins, II, 194; also in Draper Mss. 18CC130.

21 Lexington *Kentucky Gazette,* January 12, 1788; Draper Mss. 18CC130.

22 Clark, *History of Kentucky,* 304.

23 Lexington *Kentucky Gazette,* September 1, 1787. "Catholicus" was probably the pseudonym of Caleb Wallace, a former Presbyterian clergyman, who became active in political affairs. See William H. Whitsitt, *Life and Times of Judge Caleb Wallace* (Filson Club *Publications,* no. 4, Louisville, 1888).

Transylvanian"[24] deplored the influence of sectarian religion on education. They were replied to by "A Sectarian"[25] who disparaged liberalism and advocated sectarian control as the source of truth and virtue.

Filson, who was an opportunist as well as a teacher, saw in this newly aroused interest in education a means of earning a living and also of engaging in a lively controversy. He plunged in immediately, and within a few weeks after his return he had proposed to establish an academy of his own. With characteristic lack of tact he set forth the advantages of a school in town over one in the country and of the superiority of northern teachers. Also, he expressed a nonsectarian point of view. Although born into a Presbyterian family, he had lost the sectarian spirit entirely, a fact that was significant of several trends of his day. First, the Presbyterianism of the Filsons was of the "new side" or liberal variety; also, he had obviously read much in the French deistical thought that became popular in this country; and finally, Calvinism, no matter how dogmatic, has always contained the seeds of liberalism, both by its stress on individualism and also by inadvertently driving many of its own members into apostasy and rebellion.

The announcement of the opening of Filson's seminary constitutes one of the most bizarre documents in the history of American education:

The public has been informed that a seminary is proposed in Lexington. In consultation of the respectable inhabitants upon that subject, there appeared a proper spirit of encouragement: every gentleman present was suitably impressed with the importance of the plan, and seriously wished the accomplishment. Many valuable advantages will probably arise from this institution, as the situation will be popular and healthy, in the center of a fertile country, where accomodations for students may be had at the lowest rates. The teachers are determined to pay the strictest attention

[24] Lexington *Kentucky Gazette,* November 10, 1787.
[25] *Ibid.,* December 22, 1787.

Old Swede's (Holy Trinity) Church, Wilmington, Delaware,
where John Filson's parents were married in 1752
Photograph by Sanborn Studio, Wilmington

to their pupils, and hope their success will merit encouragement. With the discipline of northern teachers to suppress every species of vice and immorality, and give the greatest encouragement to the fruit and practice of virtue, party spirit will be exploded, and to instruct in the general system of Christianity only, considered as their indispensable duty.

The ideas of mankind with respect to the seats of education are various, some prefer a town or city, others the country; the latter, viewing the many temptations youths are exposed to in towns, and supposing they are fewer in the country, think that the most eligible; however probable this may appear, yet experience proves that a being, determined on folly, will find as many opportunities in the country, as in town, with the addition of a greater secresy in accomplishing his designs: many mean and vicious practices can be effected, which in a public situation the unavoidable idea of detection would effectually prevent; this obvious from a view of a country student walking out of school, he carelessly hulks his body along in clownish gestures, pays no respect to a genteel movement, from a consciousness that no eye beholds him, fears not the contempt or ridicule which must be consequent upon such a conduct in a respectable town, or if in a public situation indecorum should pass unnoticed by all, but the teachers, then is the most pertinent season for admonitions, when the culprit must be sensible upon the smallest observation of the ruinous consequences to all characters and future reputation, which he must unavoidably sustain. I conceive the voice of thunder could not make more serious impressions. Experience beyond doubt will confirm these observations.

The advantage of knowing mankind also, which those in a recluse situation can not, and after a series of time, except their studies, are mere infants, and frequently upon their first approach into public life, by awkwardness, blast all their future fame; the contrary is evident with the young gentleman educated in public life, by frequently viewing the deformity of vice, he naturally abhors it, especially where it is treated with contempt; with the knowledge of science he becomes acquainted with human nature, has a proper idea of the world, and by the time his studies are accomplished is the gentleman as well as the scholar.

This investigation may extend to every country, at present it is designed for Kentucky, in which it is sufficient to say Lexington is not the least in account for this situation.

The tuition will be five pounds per annum, one half cash the other property, good boarding, washing and lodging may be had about one mile from town for twenty or thirty [students] at nine pounds per year, and that in property, and in case of providing a bed the boarding will be eight pounds for each one. Those who wish to secure lodgings will apply to Mr. Barr and Mr. Coburn in Lexington for information.

The education will commence some time in April, and the French language will be taught, with all the arts and sciences used in academies. In the beginning of April all students will apply for entrance, as I shall be constantly in Lexington from that time. I am, with respect, the public's obedient humble servant.

John Filson[26]

So many controversial issues were raised in this article that it is surprising that it went unanswered until early in March. One who signed himself "Agricola"[27] replied in such a sarcastic and witty vein that Filson was forced to try to throw him off his humorous tack. After expressing great delight in the new seminary and declaring that all his acquaintances "are charmed and delighted with the institution, and determined to give it every encouragement," the author launches into a masterful satire:

But, here, Sir, we labor under an unhappy disadvantage. In my neighborhood all are illiterate, and unaccustomed to high, flowery language or abstruse reasoning. Your sentiments are, many of them, so new, your style is so lofty, your periods are so lengthy and crowded with such a variety of matters, your conclusions are often so remote from their premises, and relatives quite out of sight of their antecedents, that we are totally left in the maze, and the longest line of our understandings are not able to fathom the depth of such erudition. I have therefore, by the desire of my neighbors, flung those parts of your advertisement that we could not understand into a few questions.

26 *Ibid.,* January 19, 1787; Draper Mss. 18CC130-133 Durrett, *John Filson,* 117-19.

27 Lexington *Kentucky Gazette,* March 8, 1788; Draper Mss. 18CC130-133. "Agricola" was the pseudonym of Caleb Wallace.

Among the questions asked by Agricola were:

Are youth who receive their education in populous cities generally more virtuous than such as have a private education?

What peculiar charms have northern teachers to inspire virtue, suppress vice, and explode all party spirit, that southern teachers do not possess?

What is the meaning of the verb hulk?

Are young ladies, educated in the country, guilty of the sin—of hulking?

Lastly, for the benefit of such as can not give their children a public education, be pleased to point out that peculiar moment, that particular nick of time when admonition, like a thunderbolt shall knock a hulking boy out of his "awkward gestures" into a "genteel movement."

The one issue that Agricola did not raise, and one that he probably disagreed with more than any other, was that of non-sectarian instruction in religion. He was able to find enough of the ludicrous in Filson's article to discredit it without raising the religious question. Filson replied in a serious and dignified manner. That his rejoinder was one of the most deliberate actions of his life is indicated by the fact that it did not appear until more than a month later.[28] According to tradition,[29] his friend, Robert Patterson, advised him to reply briefly and vigorously to Agricola's satire:

To Agricola:

You have taken the liberty to animadvert upon the publication of the intended Seminary, proposing a few silly and impertinent questions, which I shall take no notice of. Your officious performance Reflects no reputation, indicating a Spirit of altercation, which in every attitude I view with contempt. As you have been so personal with me, you will please to leave your name with the Printer, and oblige.

John Filson[30]

28 April 19 in the Lexington *Kentucky Gazette;* Draper Mss. 18CC130-133.

29 Durrett, *John Filson,* 71.

30 *Ibid.,* 121.

Agricola replied with a sarcastic repetition of Filson's words[31] but refused to give his name. There the matter ended.

No records of Filson's seminary have been found. Actually, it is doubtful that he ever got it under way, and if he did, it had an extremely short life.[32] In view of the many other enterprises which he undertook during the spring and summer of 1788 it is not likely that he spent much time in the schoolroom. As a teacher he doubtless enjoyed the opportunity to air his views on education, but as a perennially hopeful adventurer he did not regret being free from the confining responsibilities of the classroom.

There is scant evidence of Filson's career as a schoolmaster. He is consistently referred to as a teacher, and among the pitiably few personal effects he left behind at the time of his disappearance is a textbook—*The Schoolmaster's Assistant, Being a Compendium of Arithmetic both Practical and Theoretical,* by Thomas Dilworth.[33] But as to his manner in the classroom we have no knowledge.

Outside the classroom Filson bore many of the stereotyped characteristics of the pedagogue. Pedantic, didactic, and trivial, he was often irritating and even ludicrous to his contemporaries. But he was probably not more typical of the frontier schoolmaster than he was of any of the frontiersmen. Although he was always on the verge of poverty, he was bold in his financial venture. His interests prepared him for a sedentary life, but he displayed the inexhaustible physical energy of a wilderness scout. And although he was infatuated with the raw frontier, his tastes, if somewhat baroque, remained elegant. As the first wandering intellectual in the new Kentucky settlements he was a worthy forerunner of Audubon and Rafinesque.

[31] Lexington *Kentucky Gazette,* May 17, 1788.

[32] Kentucky historians have assumed that Filson's school was a thriving institution. See, for example, Clark, 304.

[33] Preserved in the Clarke Collection.

Chapter 9 Losantiville

AS THOUGH he had some presentiment of coming events, Filson during the spring and summer of 1788 quickened his pace. The pedagogical stramash in which he was engaged in Lexington was soon forgotten, and in view of his many other activities it is hardly possible that he gave much time to educational matters. He is reported to have served as the foreman of a jury in Louisville; he continued the pioneers' search for the legendary silver mine of Swift; he advanced his knowledge of Latin; he began the study of medicine; he wrote a tristful poem of unrequited love; he surveyed a road through the wilderness from Lexington to the mouth of the Licking; and he helped found the city of Cincinnati, which he fondly named Losantiville.

Whatever the condition of his credit and however grotesque his ideas on education, Filson apparently had maintained considerable status among his contemporaries. On March 7 in Louisville he was named foreman of a jury that included several prominent citizens.[1] The case was an unusual one: a blooded mare belonging to the estate of Colonel John Floyd had wandered into the rye field of George Pomeroy, who set his venerable and ineffectual cur to drive her out of the field. The chase, which was a feeble one, had no sooner begun than Pomeroy's mongrel was joined by a bulldog that had more than an amateur's interest in the matter. He had been trained to seize cattle and horses by the nose, thereby causing them to turn somersaults. Rushing upon the mare, he caught a grip on her nose so violently that she fell over on her back and broke it. Since Pomeroy did not have the field properly fenced, he was sued for the value of the mare. Filson as foreman is reported to have persuaded the other jurors, who were disposed to award damages, that the bulldog alone was responsible for the death of the mare and that Pomeroy was in no way liable.

Along with his educational and civic activities Filson continued his scrambling pursuit of riches. The Golconda of both the Indians and the pioneers in Kentucky was a silver mine supposed to be hidden in one of the remote valleys of the eastern mountains. One John Swift was said to have mined there intermittently from 1760 to 1769 and to have cached a great quantity of ore along the banks of a mountain stream when he was forced by a band of marauding Indians to flee light-handed.[2] This story kindled and rekindled the Kentuckians' desire for wealth; and pioneers of all classes made sporadic searches for the treasure. James Harrod for one disappeared mysteriously while searching for the mine.[3] It would have been surprising indeed if Filson had not joined his contemporaries in this quest.

Filson thought that he had not only found the mine but also that he had bought it. On May 17, 1788, he and John Breckenridge entered one thousand acres which they believed included both the mine and the cache of silver:

Robert Breckenridge and John Filson as Tenents in Common, Enters 1000 acres of land upon the balance of a Treasury Warrant No. 10,117 about 60 or 70 miles North Eastwardly from Martin Cabbins in Powells Valley to include a silver mine which was Im-

1 The only authority for the following story is Durrett, *John Filson,* 75-76.
2 Collins, *History of Kentucky,* II, 414-15.
3 Mason, *James Harrod of Kentucky,* 179.

proved about 17 years ago by a Certain man named Swift at said mine the Said Swift reports he has extracted from the oar a Considerable quantity of Silver some of which he made into Dollars and left at or near the mine, together with the apperatus for making the same the same to be his in a square and the lines to run at the Cardinal points of the Camp aforesaid including the mine in the Centre as near as may be.[4]

Filson, well acquainted by this time with the uncertainty of the frontier, did not place all his hopes in a semimythical silver mine. An extraordinary candid glimpse into the variety of his enterprises can be had by a look at the meager remains of his correspondence. Only one of his personal letters of this year has been preserved. Written at Lexington on May 27 and directed to his brother Robert in Chester County, it was "to be left at the Sign of the Waggon on Lancaster road."[5] In it he reported his current activities. As usual he was trying to pay some of his debts, and he was optimistic about his prospects. He reminded his brother, who was still harassed by Filson's creditors, that he had recently sent him seventy-seven pounds, which "I suppose, with what Jordan owes answer the present exigence." He pleaded that he was doing the best he could and that one Joseph Cloud, whose son had apparently gone to Kentucky with Filson, owed him one hundred dollars.

In an earlier letter Robert had suggested that he should come out to Kentucky, probably to see for himself how his brother's affairs stood. But John discouraged him: "You write me you will come out this fall. I want you to stay until matters are settled, or go to Wilson[6] and plead time or agree to give him the rent of the plantation until paid."

4 Attested copy of the entry in Jillson, *Filson's Kentucke,* 179.

5 Original in the Clarke Collection, Ohio Historical and Philosophical Society, Cincinnati.

6 Probably the Flahavan Willson to whom Filson was indebted to the extent of 130 pounds. In 1793 Willson received from Robert Filson, as executor of John's estate, a tract of land in East Fallowfield Township for the balance owed him. Notes on the settlement of Filson's estate in the Clarke Collection.

Again, in a postscript he included information that was clearly of a nature to discourage Robert from making the trip: "The Indians are very troublesome. A few days ago Col. Joseph Mitchell, who lived at the —— Springs on Potowmack, & his —— son, fell a prey to the Savages near the falls of Ohio. We are all warriors here, when the troubles will end I know not. four boats are taken this spring by the indians."

However, despite his debts and the Indian troubles, Filson was cheerful: "I have supported a good credit here [Lexington], and have enough to support me. I resumed my Studies last winter and greatly advanced my latin, and this spring have begun to study Physic with Doctr Slater in this place, an eminent Physician who came here from London last year, two years I Study, as soon as my Study is finished I am to be married, which will be greatly to our advantage. Stand it out 2 years my dear brother, you shall have negroes to wait of you."[7]

Sometime during the spring, perhaps as late as May, Filson entered into an agreement to study medicine with one Dr. John Slater, who had recently come to Lexington from England. The articles[8] are pointlessly long and exceedingly involved. Wandering through the labyrinth of the conditions imposed on both parties, one is able to discern a few straightforward stipulations. Slater was to move a supply of medicines and pharmaceutical apparatus, including a still, from Philadelphia and to set up an apothecary shop. Filson was to be his partner and for a period of two years his student. During this time Slater was to instruct him "to the extent of his knowledge and ability, in all the knowledge, & mistery, of the theory and practice of Physic, surgery, and midwifery, also the full use of his books on Physic, Surgery, etc, during said term of two years: for which, and on account thereof, Said Filson shall

[7] When Robert Filson died in 1818, he was the owner of six slaves. Note on the settlement of his estate in the Clarke Collection.

[8] Original in the Clarke Collection.

pay Said Doctr. Slater the sum of twenty pounds as a fee, in good lands at valuable rates, not exceeding three miles from Lexington."[9]

The duration of this partnership and apprenticeship was in inverse proportion to the length of the articles of agreement. Medicine was a minor art on the frontier and its mystery there a prosy one. In the few months remaining to him Filson again became intoxicated with the possibilities of the colonization of new lands. However, before he set out for the last time to explore and to survey, Filson learned that woman as well as Fate is fickle. The solitary reference in his last letter to his forthcoming marriage and a heart-smitten poem written a few weeks later are the only records of romance in Filson's life. The first is chilling in its matter-of-fact avarice: there is no doubt that the guileless and poverty-stricken Filson was informing his brother that they both stood to profit materially from the marriage. The poem on the other hand is extravagantly romantic, but trite. Its style could be used either to express the anguish of deep disappointment or to serve as a formal expression of a passing infatuation. There are no further clues to the intensity of Filson's emotions.

The lady of property who was to become the wife of John Filson remains unknown. She has achieved a sort of immortality under the name Amanda, the name she bore in a poem written by the lovesick Filson on Beargrass Creek near Louisville.

Written at Beargrass 30th June, 1788.

Adieu ye limpid streams and cooling shades,
Adieu ye groves, ye meadows, fields and meads,
Adieu to all this scene and yon green bowers,
Adieu to sweets and all this field of flowers;
Adieu ye warbling train in every grove,
Adieu, awhile, to all on earth but love.

9 *Ibid.*

Adieu the sounding harp and cheerful lute
Adieu the viol bass or german flute.
Adieu these rural scenes that once could please,
Adieu to every joy and to my ease.
Adieu most merry dances on the green,
Adieu those blithesome hours I once have seen.
Adieu to every joy which time invades,
Adieu ye faithful swains and beauteous maids.
Adieu Amanda who my soul ensnares
Adieu till fate this mortal wound repairs.
Adieu my peace, the busy world farewell,
Adieu to all but plains of Asphodel.
Farewell yon mountains—brow and all the plain;
One leap in yonder gulf shall end my pain.
Then to Elysium fields I'll wing my way,
Through dreary wastes to reach perpetual day,
There with happy souls I'll careless rove
And in their realms forget the pains of love.[10]

But Filson did not leap. Nor apparently was he inconsolable. The "pains of love" were forgotten, not in Elysium, but across the Ohio River, where he entered upon the grandest and the last of his ventures. As early as November, 1787, Judge John Cleves Symmes of New Jersey was advertising for settlement the land between the two Miami Rivers as "equal to any part of the federal territory in point of quality of soil, and excellence of climate, it lying in the latitude of about thirty-eight degrees north, where the winters are moderate, and no extreme heats in summer. . . . There are no mountains in the tract, and, excepting a few hills, the country is generally level, and free from stone on the surface of the earth, but there are plenty of stone quarries for building. . . . For the quantity, a larger

[10] The manuscript of this poem was found about 1884 by Americus Symmes of Louisville among the papers of his father. It is in Filson's handwriting and possibly passed to Symmes by way of Judge John Cleve Symmes, a great-uncle, with whom Filson was associated in his last days. Colonel Durrett, who possessed the original, wrote that at the foot of Second Street in Louisville an old tree thrown across Beargrass Creek and serving as a bridge was called "lover's leap," either prior to or because of this poem. *John Filson,* 76-77.

proportion of the lands on the Miami are supposed to be of the first quality, and the whole equally good, compared with those of Kentucke."[11] Later, settlers were encouraged to migrate to this promised land by the offer of free lots, enough timber to build a log house, and a supply of Indian corn sufficient for six months.[12]

The lure of the West continued to attract settlers. By June, 1788, Symmes had turned over to the Treasury Board of the United States in payment on his western lands $83,333.30 in military bounties and continental certificates which he had received for land warrants.[13] Among the Jerseymen who entered land in Symmes' patent was Matthias Denman of Essex County. On a tract of almost eight hundred acres lying directly opposite the mouth of the Licking River he proposed to build a town. Preceding Symmes to the Ohio Valley—he is supposed to have arrived in July[14]—he visited the site and then went to Lexington to find partners for his enterprise. He found them in Robert Patterson and John Filson, who was then living at Patterson's house.[15] Both of these men would be valuable to the settlement. Patterson, capable, brave, and respected, had prestige with the Kentuckians; and Filson, skilled as a surveyor and persuasive in his publicity, could lay out the town and advertise it.

The covenant these three men made has been preserved:

11 John Cleve Symmes, "The Trenton Circular to the Respectable Public of November 26, 1787," *Quarterly Publication of the Historical and Philosophical Society of Ohio,* V, no. 3 (1910), 90-91. For an account of Symmes' early activity with regard to the Ohio lands, see Beverley W. Bond, Jr., *The Foundations of Ohio* (Columbus, Ohio State Archaeological and Historical Society, 1941), 290-92.

12 New Brunswick, New Jersey, *Brunswick Gazette and Weekly Monitor,* January 8, 22, 1788; quoted in Bond, *Foundations of Ohio,* 291.

13 Beverley W. Bond, Jr. (ed.), *Correspondence of John Cleves Symmes* (New York, Macmillan Company, 1926), 10-11, 30-31, 33-34.

14 Beverley W. Bond, Jr. (ed.), "Dr. Daniel Drake's Memoir of the Miami Country, 1779-1794," *Quarterly Publication of the Historical and Philosophical Society of Ohio,* XVIII (1923), 55.

15 *Ibid.*

A covenant and agreement made and concluded this 25th day of August 1788, between Matthias Denman of Essex County New Jersey State of the one part and Robert Patterson and John Filson of Lexington in Fayette County, Kentucky of the other part witnesseth; that the said Matthias Denman having made entry of a tract of land on the northwest side of Ohio river opposite the mouth of Licking river, in that district in which Judge Symmes has purchased from Congress and being seized thereof by right of entry to contain 640 acres and the fractional parts that may pertain, do grant bargain and sell the full two thirds thereof by an equal undivided right in partnership with the said Robert Patterson and John Filson their heirs and assigns; and upon producing indisputable testimony of his the said Denman's right and title to the said premises they the said Patterson and Filson shall pay the sum of £20 Virginia currency to the said Denman or his heirs or assigns as full remittance for moneys by him advanced in pay of said lands, every other institution, determination, and regulation respecting the laying off a town and establishing a ferry at and upon the premises to be the result of the united advice and consent of the parties in covenant aforesaid; and by these presents the parties bind themselves for the true performance of these covenants to each other in the penal sum of £1000 specie, hereunto affixing their hands and seals the day and year above written.

Signed sealed and delivered in the presence of Henry Owen, Abr McConnell

Matthias Denman
R. Patterson
John Filson[16]

The three partners began almost at once to promote the settlement of the town. From Lexington they hoped to attract settlers; accordingly on September 5, 1788, the following prospectus, written by Filson, appeared in the *Kentucky Gazette:*

The subscribers being proprietors of a tract of land opposite the mouth of the Licking River, on the North West side of [the] Ohio; have determined to lay off a town upon that excellent situation. The local and natural advantages speaks its future prosperity,; being equal if not superior to any, on the bank of [the] Ohio between

16 Recorded October 6, 1803, Book D-1, p. 65, Hamilton County, Ohio, Clerk's office; quoted in full from the original in Durrett, *John Filson,* 79-80.

the Miamis. The in-lotts to be each half an acre, the out-lotts four acres, thirty of each to be given to settlers, upon paying one dollar and a half for the survey and deed of each lot. The fifteenth day of September is appointed for a large company to meet in Lexington, and mark a road from there to the mouth of Licking, provided Judge Symmes arrives, being daily expected. When the Town is laid off, lots will be given to such [persons] as may become residents before the first of April next.

Matthias Denman
Robert Patterson
John Filson[17]

Symmes was late in arriving. Word reached Lexington that he would not reach the site until September 22, and a notice announcing a change in the starting day appeared in the *Kentucky Gazette* for September 13: "N. B. The time appointed to go to the mouth of Licking is put off from the 15th as published last week to the 18th inst, when a large party will start from Lexington in order to meet Judge Symmes on Monday the 22d at that place agreeable to his own appointment and the business will then go on as proposed."[18]

This second notice was signed by Patterson alone. Denman may have gone to Limestone to meet Symmes,[19] and Filson, with characteristic impatience, was reportedly on his way to the mouth of the Licking, surveying a road through the wilderness as he went. This road, which reached the mouth of the Licking in almost a straight line, is now alleged to be the route used by the Southern Railway.[20]

Symmes, after landing at Limestone, may have gone inland to Lexington.[21] In the diary of his surveyor, Israel Ludlow, whom he brought from New Jersey with him, the date of the

17 Lexington *Kentucky Gazette,* September 5, 1788; also Draper Mss. 8 00-9.
18 Quoted in Durrett, *John Filson,* 84.
19 *Ibid.*; Charles Theodore Greve, *Centennial History of Cincinnati* (2 vols., Chicago, Biographical Publishing Company, 1904), I, 163.
20 William Henry Smith, "A Pioneer Historian," *Dial,* V (1884), 133-35.
21 See Bond, "Drake's Memoir," 55.

arrival of the party at the mouth of the Licking is given as September 22:

> Sept. 20. Set out from [lower] Limestone with about 50 men—at 5 O'c'k P.M. stopt at the Station 12 miles from Limestone where staid till about 1 o'clock when we started, floated all night. Arrived at Little Miami the 22nd day about 8 oclock in the morning. The same day surveyed down as far as Licking 6 miles & 3/4—arrived at Great Miami the 25th, being 27 miles & 38 chains from Little Miami. The 23d Inst. Judge Symmes with a party of horse of about fifty from Lexington set out from Licking and travelled out to view the country and returned to the mouth of Great Miami the 28th.[22]

Patterson, Filson, and a party of Kentuckians had apparently gone to the mouth of the Licking by land,[23] where they met the Symmes party on September 22. Filson had already drawn a plat of the town,[24] but there is no conclusive evidence of how much surveying he did. According to one version, he had disappeared before he had stretched a chain on the ground.[25] Since he was of Symmes' party that left the site on September 23—the day after he is supposed to have arrived—for an exploring excursion up the Great Miami, he would scarcely have had time to run a survey. Furthermore, Patterson, perhaps to avoid legal complications, testified in 1811 that Filson had not laid out the town.[26] On the other hand, in the same year Joel Williams, one of the first lot-holders, stated in sworn testimony that on September 23 Filson had begun laying out the town, locating some of the streets as they remain today.[27]

22 *Ibid.*, 56; Draper Mss. 20125.

23 Bond, "Drake's Memoir," 55; also Greve, 167, and Greve's statement in the introduction to Symmes, "The Trenton Circular," 80. Some historians claim that the entire party assembled at Limestone and from there went down the Ohio by boat. See Henry Howe, *Historical Collections of Ohio* (3 vols., Columbus, H. Howe & Son, 1891), II, 24; Collins, II, 433.

24 Charles Cist, *The Cincinnati Miscellany* (2 vols., Cincinnati, C. Clark, 1845), I, 9.

25 *Ibid.*

26 Durrett, *John Filson*, 87.

27 *Ibid.*, 88, 123-24; also Greve, 163. "Filson spent a day or two running lines of the streets marking his course with notches in the trees."

There is no reason to doubt the statement in Ludlow's diary that Filson began his fatal trip with Symmes on September 23. However, we do not know the exact time of Filson's arrival at the mouth of the Licking. If he did arrive a day or two before the twenty-third, it would be hard to believe that he had not made a rudimentary survey.

Even before he had gone to the site, Filson had christened the new town:

> John Filson from three languages
> With pedant skill did frame
> The novel word Losantiville
> To be the new town's name.[28]

With an undoubted vision of a great western city before him, Filson had carefully coined its name. In its original form the name was Losantiburg: "Losantiburg is derived from four languages, Viz English, latin, Greek, and German and Backwards will read thus a Town opposite the mouth of the Licking."[29] But Filson soon changed it to the more euphonious Losantiville: "L for Licking River; os, Latin for mouth; anti, Greek for opposite; and ville, French for city."

Despite the preposterous pedantry of its origin, the name was good. But it was not to last. General Arthur St. Clair, who was appointed Governor of the Northwest Territory in 1787, came to Losantiville in 1790 and audaciously changed its name to Cincinnati, in honor of the Society of the Cincinnati. According to one account, when Israel Ludlow went on board the Governor's schooner, he was asked what he called his town. When he answered, "Losantiville," St. Clair exclaimed, "Give me a name I can read and write!" "Will you," said Ludlow, "please to name it?" And St. Clair answered, "Let it be Cin-

[28] From W. H. Venable's ballad on John Filson, published in *June on the Miami, and Other Poems*, Cincinnati, 1877; quoted in full by Durrett, *John Filson*, 125-28.

[29] An undated and unsigned manuscript in Filson's handwriting, Draper Mss. 2MM60.

cinnati."[30] From a letter written by Symmes on January 9, 1790, the exact date of the change is known: "Governor St. Clair arrived at Losantiville on the 2d instant. He could be prevailed to stay with us but three nights. He has organized this purchase into a county. His Excellency complimented me with the honor of naming the county. I called it *Hamilton County* after the Secretary of the Treasury. General Harmar has named the garrison *Fort Washington.* The Governor has made Losantiville the county town by the name of *Cincinnata,* so that Losantiville will become extinct."[31]

There was considerable discussion about whether the place should be called Cincinnati for members of the order or Cincinnata, "the place where the knights of the order dwell."[32] The former was accepted, and Losantiville was hurriedly forgotten.

Not content to accept the change as one justified by the pride of a general who was a new governor and a member of a new society of the officers of a new army, historians have continued to belittle the name Losantiville. One who was derisive of so pretentious a name fell into a worse pedantry by calling it "an eccentric polyglot neologism."[33] Also, the eminent John Bach McMaster used it as the subject of a charming paragraph:

Denman and Patterson were no scholars. But Filson had once been a schoolmaster, knew a little of Latin and something of his-

30 Bond, "Drake's Memoir," 74. Another version has it that when General St. Clair landed and was told the name of the town, he roared "Losantiville! What an awful name! God damn it! Call it Cincinnatti!" Alvin F. Harlow, *The Serene Cincinnatians* (New York, E. P. Dutton and Company, Inc., 1950), 23.

31 An organization formed at the close of the Revolutionary War to be composed of the officers of the Continental Army. Later officers of the navy and of the French army and navy were admitted. See Edgar Erskine Hume, "The Naming of the City of Cincinnati," *Ohio State Archaeological and Historical Quarterly,* XLIV (1935), 81-91.

32 *Ibid.*

33 Quoted in Durrett, *John Filson,* 83. See also, Charles Frederic Goss, *Cincinnati, the Queen City* (4 vols., Chicago, S. J. Clarke Publishing Company, 1912), I, 43; and Collins, II, 432.

tory, and to him was assigned the duty of choosing a name for the town. He performed the task in a way that must have excited the admiration of the humble race of pedagogues to which he belonged. The melodious Indian names were too barbarous for his scholarly taste. And as he could recall none among cities ancient or modern quite to his liking, he determined to make one, and produced a word that was a most absurd mixture of Latin, Greek, and French. He called the place Losantiville which, being interpreted, means the city opposite the mouth of the Licking. A few weeks later the Indians scalped him.[34]

One may well wonder at the historians' outraged tastes. Certainly there were many things to laugh at about poor Filson, but Losantiville is hardly one of them. The name is artificial, but so are countless other names on our land. And it is quite as euphonious as Cincinnati; and more so than Keokuk, which so far has not been changed. Perhaps General St. Clair ridiculed the name so that he could rechristen the new town, and the sycophants are still laughing. Or perhaps a conspiracy against Filson and the whole "humble race of pedagogues" continues until now.

[34] *A History of the People of the United States* (8 vols., New York, D. Appleton and Company, 1883-1913), I, 516.

Chapter 10 The Legacy

THAT THE NAME he so carefully devised for his town would be ridiculed, abandoned, and forgotten, John Filson never knew. Within a week after he arrived at the projected Losantiville he had disappeared forever, and even his own name was almost entirely forgotten for a hundred years. The circumstances of his disappearance were not heroic. From the contemporary records there are vague and fragmentary accounts of his being killed by an Indian.

The most authentic story comes from John Cleves Symmes, who a day or two after his arrival started inland to explore the country between the two Miamis. Accompanied by a party of Kentuckians, including Filson, he had gone about forty miles up the Great Miami when he encountered a band of hostile Shawnee. The Kentuckians wanted to fight, but Symmes attempted to dissuade them. As a result they became rebellious, and several of them deserted him. Filson remained with him for a while, but finally, out of fear of an Indian attack, fled toward the settlement. On the way, according to Symmes, he was killed by a lone Indian.

Here is the story in Symmes' own words, written on October 12, 1788: "I attempted to run down the great Miami from the fifth range, but being escorted by the people of Kentucky, they became disorderly & left me about one half of them & after runing down seven miles the (y) would needs go home, and for that time disappointed me. I shall however soon attempt it again, two men deserted me back in the country, & one of them Mr. Filson, publisher of the Map of Kentucky was killed in three hours after he left us, by a single Indian."[1]

Symmes referred to the death of Filson in two subsequent letters. In one written on November 25 he appeared to exonerate himself of any responsibility: "Mr. Filson deserted me when at Miami and in three hours after was shot—he then was not of my party—he would have been safe had he been."[2]

In the third letter, written on May 18 the following year, he recounted the story of the defection of the Kentuckians.

> After this, the greater part of them (the Kentuckians) deserted me when about forty miles up the Miami, where I had ventured on their promises to escort me down that river, meandering its courses; which so disobliged me that I have been very indifferent ever since whether one of them came into the purchase or not, as I found them very ungovernable and seditious; and not to be awed or persuaded. To the disobedience of these men, I impute the death of poor Filson, who had no rest afterwards while with me, for fear of the Indians, and at length attempting to escape to the body of men I had left on the Ohio, he was destroyed by the savages.[3]

Another contemporary account varies in some detail from that left by Colonel Symmes. Ludlow's diary, which refers to the Symmes expedition into the country north of the Ohio, says that Symmes returned to the mouth of the Great Miami on November 28, "and brought us the news of Mr. Filson being shot by an Indian."[4]

The story is told again in the oft-quoted Garrard letter: "The party with whom John Filson was in company was attacked by the Indians on the big Miami it is supposed near where Miami Town now stands. The party had dismounted

[1] Letter of John Cleves Symmes to Jonathan Dayton, dated at Limestone, October 12, 1788. Taken from Bond, *Correspondence of John Cleves Symmes,* 46.

[2] *Ibid.,* 52; to Jonathan Dayton. [3] *Ibid.,* 70; to Jonathan Dayton.

[4] Bond, "Drake's Memoir," 56.

from their horses and were gathering plums where the Indians made the attack. Two guns were fired by the Indians when each one made for their horses. Filson was one of the hindmost of the party or nearest the Indians and he was never heard from afterwards."[5]

There are other, briefer accounts. An old, time-stained letter written in Fayette County on October 11, 1788, by an unknown hand and addressed to Captain McDowell in Richmond, Virginia, concludes with these words: "I have nothing new to inform you of except Mr. Filson being killed over the Ohio River."[6] Joseph Buell, a sergeant stationed at Ft. Harmar at the mouth of the Muskingum, entered in his journal under the date of October 21, 1788, the following item: "Four canoes landed from Kentucky, loaded with ginseng; and report that the Indians had attacked a party of men with Judge Symmes, and killed one of his surveyors."[7] Another, more loving hand recorded the mournful event in one of the schoolmaster's textbooks. In a copy of *The Schoolmaster's Assistant* Robert Filson wrote: "This Book was given to me by my Brother John Filson, who was kill'd by an Indian on the West Side of the Ohio, October the first 1788, about 5 miles from the Great Miami River, and 20 or 25 from the Ohio."[8] These are the terse obituaries for one whose style had been fulsome.

Despite the unanimity of the contemporary accounts that John Filson was killed by an Indian, doubts as to the manner

[5] *Ibid.*, 96-97; Draper Mss. 10lo7. J. D. Garrard, a lawyer, abridged an affidavit from Denman, about 1827. Denman's statement, made many years after the event, probably should not be given the same weight as Symmes'. However, the fact that he gave the details more clearly than Symmes might indicate that he witnessed the circumstances of Filson's separation.

[6] Among the Shane Papers in the Presbyterian Historical Society, Witherspoon Building, Philadelphia; quoted by Wilson, "John Filson in Pennsylvania," 194.

[7] Collins, *History of Kentucky,* II, 433, quotes this as 1789, but Durrett, *John Filson,* 91, has it 1788.

[8] In the Clarke Collection, Ohio Historical and Philosophical Society, Cincinnati. If the statement in Ludlow's diary that Symmes returned to the mouth of the Great Miami on September 28 and reported the death of John Filson is true, then Filson was killed on or before that date.

of his disappearance have persisted.[9] Apparently no white man witnessed his death, his remains were never found, and the Indians as well as the forests kept the secret. The red men were continuing in their hostility to the encroaching white settlers, and so vicious were their attacks that year that the site of Losantiville was known as the "Miami slaughterhouse."[10] In this land of bold warriors, white and red, Filson fell a martyr to the lesser arts of surveying and pedagogy.

> Then come, ye pedagogues, and join
> To sing and graceful lay
> For him the martyr pioneer
> Who led for you the way[11]

Two melancholy facts appear immediately after Filson's death: he had paid nothing on his purchase of a third interest in Losantiville; and he was scarcely missed. On October 5 Matthias Denman wrote to Robert Patterson:

> As you are fully acquainted with the fate of Mr. Filson and as you are fully acquainted that I have not been paid according to Contract and by Agrement you are Bound to me on Mr. Fillsons accompt fifty Dollars for the Section and so in proportion for the fractions which from the survey made Mr. Ludlow appear to amount to [a] full Section more the whole Amounts to one Hundred Dollars after having taken the best Opinion I have Agreed that if the money is not paid before I go up the River which will be about the 13th Inst. I shall cansell the Obligation and take in another partner in order that we may form the settlement.[12]

Denman and Patterson admitted Israel Ludlow, Symmes' surveyor, as a partner, and Filson's rights in Losantiville were lost to his heirs at law.[13] Years later, sworn testimony was given that these three men ransacked Filson's trunk and destroyed his

[9] Durrett was inclined to accept the story, *John Filson,* 96; but see Draper Mss. 8CC9; Bond, *The Foundations of Ohio,* 293; and Greve, *Centennial History of Cincinnati,* I, 164.

[10] John C. Hover, and others (eds.), *Memoirs of the Miami Valley* (3 vols., Robert O. Law Company, Chicago, 1919), I, 27-28.

[11] Venable's ballad.

[12] Draper Mss. 2MM57.

[13] Durrett, *John Filson,* 124. See also, Cist, *The Cincinnati Miscellany,* I, 9.

papers in order to defraud his heirs.[14] But this evidence, if true, came too late to change the swiftly moving course of the original titles to the lands in the Miami Purchase. Careless while living, the dead Filson could hardly be expected to hold the title until his heir arrived from Chester County. Grasping hands had seized his rights as soon as he disappeared.

To patient Robert Filson, still living on his farm in Chester County, fell the final duty of settling his brother's estate. John Filson was a legal resident of Pennsylvania, and he had left a will in Chester County, which he had drawn on November 21, 1786:

In the name of God amen, I John Filson of East Fallowfield township in Chester County, State of Pennsylvania being in perfect health and sound memory, and Calling to mind the mortality of my body, knowing it is appointed for all men once to die, do Constitute, make and ordain this my last Will, and Testament in manner and form following Viz, I first and principally, Commend my soul to God who gave it, hopeing to receive the same again at the genneral resurrexion, My body I also commend to the Care of providence, and the discretion of my friends or fellow Creatures, to be buried in a Christian like manner. . . . And as to such worldly substance wherewith it hath pleased God to bless me, I give and bequeath the whole and every part thereof, both real and personal to my dear brother Robert Filson and his heirs for ever Viz five hundred acres of Land in Jefferson County in Virginia and one thousand acres in the same County and State as will appear due from Squire Boone of Sd. County upon two Certain bonds to John Kephart which Sd. bonds were assigned to me, also all the propriety of the lands entered on big bone and Stepstone Creeks, as will appear by entries in Colo. Marshal's office in Fayette County in Virginia affores'd, also all the amount of bonds due to me in Kentucke & recovering by law, as will appear by a list thereof in the hands of Capt'n James Patton my attorney at the falls of Ohio, also all the amount of my property in Post St. Vincent, as will appear by a list of notes deeds and &c in the hands of Colo. John Small my attorney in Sd. town of St Vincents, hereby Constituteing and ordaining my brother Robert Filson affores'd, my true and lawful

[14] Durrett, *John Filson,* 124.

Executor of all my my estate both real and personal and by his discretion to be ordered as may be most Just and equitable in every of my affaires wherewith he is or may be acquainted in Witness whereof I have to these presents Set my hand and Seal ordaining as affores'd, this to be my last Will and testament & no other hereby revoking & disanuling all other will or wills heretofore made by me. Signed Sealed & delivered this 21st [*20th*] day of Nov'r. A.D. 1786.

In presence of John Filson (*Seal*)
Mary Hartt Bryan McCune
[*Sworn*] [*Sworn*] [*Invy. 1 Mo.*] [*Proven 28 Novr. 1788*][15]

By November 28, this will was proved in court, for on the back of it these words are written: "Westchester—Nov'r. 28, 1788. Then personally appeared Mary Hart & Bryan McClure and on their solemn oaths according to Law did declare, depose and say that they were personally present and did see & hear John Filson the Testator within named sign, seal publish pronounce and declare the within instrument of writing as and for his last Will and Testament and that at the doing thereof he was of a sound and well disposing mind and memory to the best of their understandings. Sworn before ——."[16] On December 8 an inventory of the worldly goods of John Filson was filed in the Court of Chester County:

An inventory and appraissement of all the goods and Chattels of John Filson, Deceased, made by us the Subscribers, this second day of December, 1788—

To A Dictionary	0	7	6
Buchan's Family Medicle book	0	7	6
To 2 Hym books	0	5	0
To Book accomp	2	1	5

Examined by us

Jos. Leonard
John Worth.

15 File no. 3985, Register of Wills, West Chester, Pennsylvania.

16 In Will Book H, vol. 8, pp. 261, 262, where the will is recorded. After the words "Sworn before," the words are subscribed—"Pers'r. Frazer, Reg'r." See Wilson, 191.

The Settlement bears the following endorsement:

Acco't. of Admini'r.—Jno. Filson's Estate—filed 21st of Dec'r., 1790.

Settlement

Acco't. of Robert Filson, Ex'cutor of the Last Will & Testament of John Filson, Deseast'd. [*sic*] as well of all & singular the Goods and Chattels, rights & Credits of the said deceast'd [*sic*] that Came to his hand as of the payments Disbursment thereunto—

Imprimis—

The said accomptant Charges himself with all & Singular the Goods & Chattels, Rights & Credits of the said Dec'asd mentioned & specified in an Inventory and appraisement thereof made & executed into the Reg'r's, office at—

	£	s.	d.
The amount of 'Praisement	3	1	5
By Cash from Jonathan Rumford, Merchant in Wilmington, August 11th, 1790,	123	1	0
	£126	2	5
Balance due the Executor	208	6	6
	£334	8	11

Errors Excepted, West Chester, 21st Decem'r., 1790.

Robert Filson.

Item—

The said accomptant prays allowance of the following payments & disbursements—

	£	s.	d.
1—Pr. Certificate from the Supreme Courtt of Kentucke after settlement	280	6	7
2—paid Daniel Jenefer Addams, Merchant in in Wilmington—August 11th, 1790,	28	13	7
3—paid Wm. Pluright of Wilmington	0	3	9
	£309	3	11
By Register's fees in Settlement Commiss'ns pr. agreement	25	5	0
	£334	8	11 [17]

The cryptic accounts speak for themselves. A few old books, some debts, and apparently an expensive litigation constituted

[17] Published in full in Wilson, 195-96.

the legacy of John Filson. In Kentucky his land warrants were lost: "in the merciless scramble of one for another's lands, the titles of Filson, without his presence to explain and enforce them, were swept away like chaff before the whirlwind."[18] And his brother was required to pay the courts in Kentucky the substantial sum of 280 pounds.

Early in 1789 Robert Filson came to Losantiville to see what he could salvage of his brother's interest in the city. But he never had an opportunity to claim or to forfeit his rights. Ludlow had been recognized as the new partner, and Filson's claim had been transferred to him. Robert Filson apparently acquiesced. Years later, the heirs of Israel Ludlow filed a petition in the Cincinnati courts against John Kidd and Joel Williams for the recovery of a lot. The defendants in their reply challenged the rights of Ludlow:

> And they further aver that the said John Filson did not at any time prior to his death sell or in any manner dispose of his right purchased from the said Matthias [Denman] as aforesaid, or any part thereof, either to the said Israel Ludlow or any other person, but that he died possessed of all the right he had acquired by virtue of the aforesaid contract with the said Matthias whereupon all the right and title of the said John Filson descended and became vested in his heirs at law who, as these defendants are informed and believe, reside in some of the Eastern States. And these defendants further state that shortly after the death of the said John Filson the said Matthias Denman, Robert Patterson, and Israel Ludlow entered into a combination, as these defendants are informed and believe, to defraud the heirs of the said John Filson of the right he had acquired in his lifetime by virtue of the before mentioned contract with the said Matthias. . . . And in pursuance of said unjust, wicked and fraudulent combination, the said Israel did usurp the right which belonged to the said John Filson at the time of his death, and did act as proprietor of one third part of the said premises.[19]

But Robert Patterson, an honorable man, twice gave testi-

[18] Durrett, *John Filson,* 100.

[19] July 25, 1811; quoted *ibid.,* 124.

mony in explanation of why Filson's heirs were not entitled to the third interest in Losantiville. First on December 27, 1803: "I was acquainted with the Brother of the said Filson who was heir at law to the said Filson and he informed me that as the said John Filson had paid nothing for the said land he did not set up any claim to the said town or consider himself as having any interest or concern therein."[20] And again on January 6, 1814:

> Matthias Denman purchased of John C. Symmes a section and fraction opposite the mouth of Licking, containing somewhere about 710 acres, and admitted this deponent and one Filson as partners in said purchase; that they agreed to lay out a town on said tract shortly afterwards, and before the town was laid off Filson was killed by the Indians; that he never had advanced or paid any money for his proportion of said tract either to Symmes or Denman, and after his death Israel Ludlow was by the consent of the other proprietors admitted an equal partner in said purchase.[21]

However, as late as November 26, 1794, Patterson in the transfer of his third interest in Cincinnati to Samuel Freeman recited, with Israel Ludlow as a witness, that Matthias Denman, Robert Patterson, and John Filson "are partners in common tenetry." It is possible that this passage read in context would mean that they *were* partners.

The facts appear to be clear. Filson had paid nothing on his contract, and when he disappeared, another surveyor was needed. Denman, in his impatience to get on with the settlement, brought Israel Ludlow, Symmes' surveyor and a fellow Jerseyman, in as the third partner. The regular, and perhaps decent, procedure would have been to give Filson's heir a chance to claim his interest. But Robert Filson was far away in Chester County and Ludlow was on the scene. Furthermore, although

[20] Hamilton County Recorder's Office, Book D-1, p. 74; Greve, 164; and Goss, *Cincinnati, the Queen City,* 48.

[21] Quoted in Durrett, *John Filson,* 125. Recorded December 29, 1811; quoted in Goss, 48.

Filson was extremely useful, his interests were not taken seriously by his partners. And while the fairness, or even the legality, of their action may be questioned, the charge of fraudulent behavior may be extreme under the circumstances.[22]

With the closing of these last accounts Filson passed into almost complete oblivion. His contemporaries were not interested in perpetuating his memory: neither city nor town, river nor county, bears his name. And although the Kentuckians have searched the histories and the heavens for names for their highways, inns, thoroughbreds, and bourbons, they have never adopted the name of their first historian and cartographer. Only in the Filson Club,[23] a historical society organized one hundred years after his *Kentucke* was published, has John Filson a fitting memorial.

Because he has received such shabby treatment, Filson's few biographers have attempted to make recompense.[24] In so doing, they have attributed to him qualities that he did not possess. In any calm and dispassionate appraisal of Filson one cannot say that he was a great man. Even allowing for his youth—he disappeared in his mid-thirties—he was impetuous, restless, impractical, pompous, and trivial. Above all he was unfortunate. Plunging repeatedly into the midst of great events, he was always forced to their periphery. So often he came so near to prominence that one can only wonder why he failed and failed again: "He (Filson) came so near to being the most fascinating character in the whole history of our city (Cincinnati) that one is tempted to meditate upon the narrow margin by which he failed. He needed, in the first place, a little more of the divine afflatus and, in the second place, to have died in some

22 For a contrary opinion, see Durrett, *John Filson,* 95-100.

23 Organized by Colonel Reuben Durrett and other prominent citizens of Louisville on May 15, 1884. Located at 118 West Breckinridge Street, it has published numerous works on Kentucky history, and it continues to publish an excellent history quarterly. See Rothert, *The Filson Club and Its Activities;* also *Filson Club Quarterly,* II (1932), no. 1.

24 Jillson, *Filson's Kentucke,* 149.

valiant personal encounter before the eyes of reliable witnesses to have rendered him our patron saint."[25]

Failing of greatness individually, Filson was one of many who made up the composite greatness of the old frontier. Warriors, heroes, statesmen there are on the tapestry of the Kentucky epic; but many lesser figures crowd into the grand design: the other Boone with the incredible name of Squire; Audubon, the painter of birds; and the rococo figure of John Filson. Each in his own way supports the main theme.

A man does not have to be great to be important. As an entrepreneur Filson was a failure. As a person he was uncongenial. And as an intellectual he was undistinguished. But because he undertook some tedious and petty tasks, he made a substantial contribution to American history and letters: his book and map sped the settlement of the West; in his tale of the adventures of Daniel Boone he created the prototype of our national hero; and as a wandering schoolmaster he carried the perennial aspirations of his kind for the spread of learning and enlightenment to the frontier. Such is the complexity of history.

[25] Goss, 43.

Index